A Real-World Guide to
Restorative Justice in Schools

A Real-World Guide to Restorative Justice in Schools

PRACTICAL PHILOSOPHY, USEFUL TOOLS,
AND TRUE STORIES

Nicholas Bradford
and
David LeSal

Jessica Kingsley Publishers
London and Philadelphia

First published in Great Britain in 2021 by Jessica Kingsley Publishers

An Hachette Company

1

Copyright © Nicholas Bradford and David LeSal 2021

Figure on p.58 reproduced with kind permission of Jon Kidde.

Front cover image source: Dreamstime.

A CIP catalogue record for this title is available from the
British Library and the Library of Congress

ISBN 978 1 78775 571 0
eISBN 978 1 78775 572 7

Printed and bound in the United States by West Publishing Corp

Jessica Kingsley Publishers' policy is to use papers that are natural, renewable
and recyclable products and made from wood grown in sustainable
forests. The logging and manufacturing processes are expected to conform
to the environmental regulations of the country of origin.

Jessica Kingsley Publishers
Carmelite House
50 Victoria Embankment
London EC4Y 0DZ

www.jkp.com

Contents

Part II: Never Forget Where You Came From

Part III: Circle Up

Acknowledgments

Nicholas
I have deep gratitude, respect, and love for the huge Restorative Justice community. Whether you know it or not there are many who breathed life into this book, to name a few: Dominic Barter, Jon Kidde, Fania Davis PhD, David Yusem, Sue Miglino, the men and staff at the Return House, Molly Rowan Leech, and Howard Zehr. In addition, it is impossible to put into words my continued amazement at the indigenous peoples around the world who held this work for generations in the face of violence and oppression. Without you our world would be lesser. I know we can do better.

To my parents, Richard and Julia Munoz Bradford, and brothers, Christopher and Andreas, who challenge me and support me at every turn. Our family of educators has been a powerful force for my own work, thank you. To my grandfather, Antonio Fernandez, your indomitable Aztec spirit runs through my veins.

And last but certainly not least my wife, Jamie, who through all this has been a rock and support from the very beginning. Together we are raising a beautiful little boy and hope together with this book and all of you, he can grow up in a kinder, more connected world.

David
I would like to give thanks to my parents, whose incredible love and support allowed me the life and education that I am privileged

to have. And to my awesome wife, who supported the writing of this book, especially during the uniquely stressful time of a global pandemic; I cannot thank you enough.

I am also indebted to the many authors, educators, and students that have shaped my knowledge and experience as an RJ facilitator. I am particularly grateful to early mentors and edu-heroes Javier Guzman, Loren Demeroutis, and Jeff Petty, whose bold leadership has inspired me.

The incredible staff and student body at Highline Big Picture High School, and in particular, an advisory project by my former student Ryan Thon, which first drew me into this important work. This is also where I met Nicholas. I would not be where I am today without those experiences and relationships.

This book has also benefited a great deal from interviews with RJ practitioners from around the country and I am humbled to be part of such a rich network of people who care so deeply about student success and wellbeing, healthy school environments, and equitable communities.

About the Authors

Nicholas Bradford was a certified teacher in Vermont and hails from Washington via California. He is the son of mixed race parents. His dad is descended from Polish immigrants and French (Canadian) trappers. Nicholas remembers very clearly the very best Polish sausages coming from the community smokehouse outside of Houston, TX. His mom is descended from Mexican/Californian and Native American (Navajo) people. His great-grandmother didn't claim Mexican heritage but instead claimed Californian heritage, as the family was in the region long before California was a state. He has deep roots in the immigrant experience and has struggled to find his ethnic/racial identity. Nicholas has one older brother and two precocious nieces.

Nicholas received his BA from Evergreen State College and his Master's Degree in Education Policy from the University of Washington. His family instilled a great value in education. During his childhood, between the years of three to seven, his mother attended university, raised two children, and worked evenings at Pizza Hut. His dad often worked two or three jobs—his full-time job was working nights as a custodian at a community college. His dad valued education, exposed him to Nova and Discovery shows at a young age, read interesting books, and introduced him to professors. While his parents were able to demonstrate through their actions that education is incredibly important, he was unsure (as many are) of how to pay for the costs of attending university after high school.

He made a life-changing decision at the age of 19 to join the United States Coast Guard Reserve, although little did he know that there would be a fair amount of active duty. After his freshman year he attended boot camp, something that is seared into the minds of any who had that opportunity. It was one of many formative experiences in the CG. He deployed twice, first on 9/11 2001 to Washington State in support of Operation Enduring Freedom and again in 2003 to Kuwait and Iraq in support of Operation Iraqi Freedom. As a young man who opposed the war it was hard to reconcile the "order" and supporting his team members who were being deployed into harm's way. This is an example of holding two contradictory things at the same time:

> I don't want to support the bombing of the Iraqi people or the invasion of a country, and I can't leave as my comrades are heading into danger.

Years later Nicholas became a teacher in New York and Vermont, and enjoyed working with "challenging" youth, youth who had been unsuccessful in traditional education settings. He believes this is because of his own non-traditional successful schooling. Working with young people who just want to be heard and valued was, and continues to be, a powerful driver for him.

David LeSal is a certified high school ELA (English language arts) teacher with over 10 years' experience in classrooms, and originally hails from New York State.

David was born the son of an agnostic Jewish father raised in Brooklyn and a devout Catholic mother from rural Massachusetts. Feeling a lack of acceptance from either religion led to an early sense of "otherness," leading to an interest in, and a search for, personal identity, culture, and spirituality. Both sides of David's family tree have roots in Russia and Poland. Despite their differing backgrounds, David's parents shared and fostered similar values of love, family, and education.

Both David's parents were teachers in low-income urban schools, subsequently working within New York State maximum security prisons as educators, mentors, and administrators. Hearing stories about, and sometimes seeing scenes from within, various prisons made clear to him the entrenched issues of racism, class-ism, and hopelessness in the criminal justice system. These stories, and his parents' stories, also provided examples of people working tirelessly and compassionately to make a difference in the lives of individual inmates.

After completing a BA at McGill University in Montreal, Canada, David earned an MFA in Creative Writing/Poetry and formally began teaching as an adjunct professor at City College of New York. While earning his Master's degree he spent almost three years as a substitute teacher throughout New York City (NYC) public schools. This "jumping into the deep end" of classroom management helped him to discover his natural love for working with middle and high school-aged students, but also exposed some of the greatest failings of many lower-income traditional schools as he spent time working and talking with the students he encountered each day. Ironically, these were many of the same issues that existed in the prisons he had been exposed to during his youth.

Drawing on a love of hip hop music, David created an after-school rap writers club at a school in Brooklyn that caught the attention of a young and ambitious new principal who would eventually offer him a job at one of NYC's first Big Picture Learning (BPL)[1] public high schools. David fell in love with the model's focus on internships, student projects, exhibitions, and advisory culture, and remained working at BPL-affiliated schools on the East and West Coast.

It was at Highline Big Picture High School in the Seattle area that he first encountered RJ philosophy and where he also met Nicholas Bradford, who would serve as his mentor and eventually as his colleague. As their work in this area progressed, Nicholas

---

[1]   www.bigpicture.org

as a trainer and David as an RJ dean in the Bronx, they kept in touch and would eventually partner together in the creation and development of the National Center for Restorative Justice (NC4RJ), providing training and resources to practitioners, educators, students, and others looking to grow their own practice.

David and Nicholas began working together in the Seattle area of Washington State, integrating their past experiences, and sharing a love for including students' voices into their RJ work. They continued to share resources and ideas over the next few years, and as Nicholas launched the NC4RJ in 2016, David joined as a training course facilitator, eventually becoming the education director. They now deliver training on RJ and practices, circles, equity, and a host of other transformative topics based on many of the concepts and tools contained in this book. You will find a great deal of encouragement, practical tools, and insightful stories in the pages that follow. We hope you love it.

Introduction

Whether you are new to the concept of restorative justice and practices, or have already developed your practice over many years, there are a ton of reasons to love this work. From decreasing the need for suspensions, and other forms of traditional discipline, to improving the health of your school community and increasing academic outcomes, the benefits of shifting to a restorative mindset are well established and taking root across America. That is not to say that implementing these practices, like all work that is important, doesn't come without difficult challenges, and a need for some tough conversations within the community.

We believe that restorative justice (RJ) can be an avenue to increasing happiness and success in everyday relationships and within significant conflict. We also know, however, that the methods in this book are not the only way to think about or work with RJ; but we believe the framework we present here provides an easily applied way of thinking about different educational settings. This includes traditional K-12 schools (from kindergarten to 12th grade), alternative schools, pre-kindergarten, as well as post-secondary education settings.

As the founder (Nicholas Bradford) and education director (David LeSal) of the National Center for Restorative Justice (NC4RJ), we have had the privilege of engaging hundreds of staff, students, and families in learning about this important work. This book contains some of the most useful and powerful tools that we use in our trainings, and we hope that it may serve as a valuable resource to anyone looking to bring about positive change in their classrooms, schools, and indeed, relationships.

Our goal is to provide you with the very best tools and insights from our years of facilitating RJ trainings with passionate educators and our reflections from working directly with students. We will provide clear and helpful foundational philosophy that will guide your growth as RJ practitioners alongside real-world examples of what this evolving craft actually looks like when put to the test in classrooms and beyond. We have divided the book up into three parts. In the first part, we look at the importance of human relationships, and outline the five main principles of RJ. We also explore conflict and restorative language, vulnerability and cultural competency. We end the first part by suggesting ways to engage resistant staff. In the second part we explore the roots of RJ, and address the vital issue of "equity." We offer resources and discussion of circles as a restorative tool in the final section.

This book is designed to clearly illustrate the many facets of building and maintaining a healthy, restorative ecosystem, while providing concrete tools and real-world stories to help guide your process and self-reflection. These stories were written and edited by David LeSal based on interviews with real-world practitioners. All student names have been changed for the purpose of these stories, and some events are a composite of multiple occasions.

PART I

DIVE DEEP

1

Relationships

THE FOUNDATION OF A RESTORATIVE ECOSYSTEM

There is a reason that this topic kicks off the journey of this book. Relationships really are the keystone of any restorative ecosystem, and especially in schools. What we know and believe 100 percent is that we are better, healthier, and stronger when we are in a relationship, when we have a connection with others. Evidence has shown that long-lasting relationships are a key indicator and driver of happiness, and not only facilitate the healing that RJ calls for, but also actually prevent harm from occurring in the first place.

As human beings we are absolutely driven to make connections and feel a belonging to a tribe or a group. Many schools could do a better job at driving home the concept "you belong here," especially for students who may not "fit the mold" and who can get lost, fall through the cracks, and feel disconnected to their school. If we don't offer those opportunities for students to connect to school, conversations with caring staff, sports teams, clubs, and activities, someone else will fill that need for connections. So often this can be gangs, unhealthy or extreme groups, or other negative influences such as drugs and crime. Forming those deep, authentic bonds with those around us creates that sense of community buy-in, and the ability to bring folks together to repair harm when it occurs and ultimately stay connected to healthy institutions.

A lack of quality relationships is also where even the best intentions can fail to cause the restorative shift and positive benefits being sought through restorative practices.

It comes down to a reframing of the idea. We must move from:

A *rule* has been broken, and something must be done *about* it.

To

A *relationship* has been harmed within the *community*, and something must be done to *repair* it.

Note that both approaches acknowledge that the harmful decision was unacceptable and both statements demand a consequence, but the framing is quite different. The first approach is often seen as "easier." After all, it doesn't require the building of relationships ("Just give me your student ID # and I can assign you a suspension"), and there is a clear-cut one-size-fits-all prescription for what to do that is quite time-efficient: "You broke rule A, so you get X number of days suspension." In fact, it would seem like this approach would produce an even more equitable system—when anyone breaks that rule, they get the same punishment—makes sense, right? So why does it turn out to be so different? Why are students of color, differently abled, LGBTQ+, and other minority groups receiving suspensions at a higher rate than their white counterparts (that do not also belong to a marginalized group) for the same offenses?[1] And furthermore, why are these punishments not changing the behaviors and leading to more academic success for all?

If traditional discipline was working (for all), we wouldn't be writing this book as there would be no a nationwide call for discipline reform, for a reduction in suspensions, an increase in equity, and for all the transformation that RJ promises.

School leaders will often ask us how quickly they can start doing

---

[1] Losen, D., Hodson, C., Keith II, M.A., Morrison, K., and Belway, S. (2015) Are We Closing the School Discipline Gap? Los Angeles, CA: The Civil Rights Project. Available at: www.civilrightsproject.ucla.edu/resources/projects/center-for-civil-rights-remedies/school-to-prison-folder/federal-reports/are-we-closing-the-school-discipline-gap/AreWeClosingTheSchoolDisciplineGap_FINAL221.pdf

RJ circles or conferences (often to reduce the rate of suspensions) when a harm occurs. The language we use here is important: *when a harm occurs*. This is already a restorative mindset shift. More often we will hear someone ask how to respond restoratively *when a rule is broken* or *when a student misbehaves*. Note that this will always be about a *student* breaking a rule or school value, never about a staff member breaking a rule or school value. And this type of question that we get asked, how to simply air-drop restorative circles into an existing school program that is otherwise not connected and restorative, reveals a great deal of what a lot of folks misunderstand about this work. It is not something to be implemented, top-down, and placed on students. When done correctly, it is a community-wide movement of accountability, vulnerability, equality, and, most of all, a movement based on the day-in, day-out building of positive and honest relationships that permeate all aspects of life.

A point of clarity: we are restoring *relationships*, and not the *status quo*

Another misunderstanding is that RJ refers to *restoring* the status quo after a harm occurs. This idea, rightly, leads many to argue that we should not be restoring a system that is racially biased, where discipline is disproportionately administered, and one in which schools are more segregated and unequally funded than ever. These reactions are both factually true and of great concern to all of us doing this work. And it is also the reason you may hear some people call for *transformative justice* to radically change the current system into one that is more fair, equitable, and inclusive. We love this term and the intention behind it, because RJ is absolutely a tool for transforming our communities in these ways. However, when we refer to RJ, we are actually not referring to restoring the status quo of an unjust system that is failing many, despite the unbelievable hard work and good intentions of teachers all across the country; we are referring to restoring *relationships*. This is a hugely important point so we will state it again: the *goal of RJ is to build, maintain, and repair relationships* within a school or community. Without existing relationships, there is nothing to repair after a harm occurs. There is no empathy, no buy-in from students or staff, no vulnerability, and no trust. This is often why attempts at RJ fail to produce positive benefits. And believe us, the positive benefits to a school community from holistically implementing RJ are huge. Being part of a restorative school can prevent drop-outs, bullying, increase test scores, reduce staff turnover, and literally save lives. We have seen this with our own eyes, and that is why we are passionate about sharing this work.

Without quality relationships, which are *earned* over time, you may find yourself sitting in a circle conference with a student saying, "Your actions greatly impacted Mr Johnson's class," and you may hear in response, "I don't care about Mr Johnson," or even worse, "Who is Mr Johnson?" If you want RJ, start by building community. If you want restorative conferences to go well after a harm has occurred, you need to have tons of opportunity for community-building circles *before* a harm occurs. Many of us have seen this type of breakdown occur, when a circle is convened with a student who just doesn't feel connected, and it goes horribly. Maybe there is an outburst of anger, complete silence, or a total lack of taking accountability. And, of course, this is an indicator that the relationship-building work with this student is not where it needs to be for the process to be successful. This is okay—circles will not always work out the way we might like them to, and we can circle back and try new ways to work with that student. But we consider ourselves extremely lucky to have seen, on countless occasions, even a severe harm dealt with in effective and powerful circles that are transformative for everyone in attendance, where students recognize the impact of their actions, take accountability, offer authentic remorse and apology, and dedicate themselves to taking measurable actions that will repair relationships.

Perhaps even more inspiring are the times that relationships prevent a harm from even occurring at all.

David says...

I ran an advisory class that benefited a great deal from almost daily community-building circles. Of course we weren't all one big happy family, as they say; we had our conflicts and students still formed cliques. One day, two friends from one clique had a heated argument, one student actually tearing his shirt off ready to throw a punch, when two students from the class, from a totally different clique and background, students who rarely interacted except for in our circles and community-building activities, grabbed the student up in a bear hug and prevented the fight, saying things like, "Bro, I'm not gonna let you do this" and "Cool off for a minute, think this through." They didn't want to see such a breakdown and violence in our advisory class. In an age where in many schools students would have been whipping out their phones to record and cheer on such a fight, I think this was a true victory and testament to our teambuilding as a group, not to mention the incredible character of those students who intervened.

Another example of relationships replacing the need for traditional discipline comes from that same advisory class. We had a student move to our relatively rural community from a dense urban neighborhood out of state. He arrived guarded and dismissive, and I could tell that he just felt like he did not belong with us. This led to several small harmful actions such as rude comments, refusing to do group work, and cutting class. I'm sure almost every teacher has had a student like this, attending the class periodically, wanting to graduate, but totally unconnected and resistant to offers of help. It can be very uncomfortable. Rather than simply taking the disciplinary route of punishing him for school rules he had broken, I took an opportunity to address the class on a day that he was absent. This was a tricky process that I felt we were ready for as a group. I told them that I wanted to respectfully discuss this student, and, especially because he was not present, we had to be very careful how we spoke. But I explained that I believed we were stronger as a group when everyone was present, and how I had lain awake at nights wondering how I could have done better at including and welcoming this student to our class (modeling vulnerability and accountability). I said that I wanted us to work as a group to think of ways that we could help him integrate into our advisory class and find academic success. Many of the students wanted to and were able to vent and share their specific frustrations for how this student had been acting, and I think that was needed—creating a safe place to discuss the impact of his choices was important to all students feeling heard. (Of course, a circle with the student present to hear these impacts could have occurred as well, but this was the route I had decided we would take at this juncture in time.) Then, as a group, we began to think out how we could take action from a place of "you belong here." Many students did not have any ideas or did not wish to help this student, especially those who had felt harmed by him, but three or four really liked this idea and offered some great suggestions. They said to me: "We should throw him a party! Just make him know that we want him here." And so that's what they did. One girl baked a cake with his name on it and brought balloons. We kept the cake in the fridge and when he showed up (late) two days later, they dropped what they were doing and ran to get the cake and balloons. He was, of course, a bit shocked, but definitely had a smile breaking through on his face as he struggled to find how to understand this loving reaction from a community he had clearly antagonized. It was a powerful moment. This student had many ups and downs over the years afterwards (life is rarely a Hallmark movie), but I strongly believe this, and other acts of connection and kindness from our school community, was a huge part of the reason he was still with us for senior year.

Building relationships... even when the going gets tough

We have said that RJ is largely about building relationships, but it is really not just about this. Rather, it is about how to build them *while* we are in or experiencing conflict. Many teachers, for instance, are great at building relationships with students who show up regularly and meet their expectations. They may be fun and engaging lecturers and have awesome learning activities planned; most teachers are passionate and excellent at their jobs after all. But when faced with students who fail to meet their expectations, who are often involved in a bevy of their own conflicts outside of the classroom, these relationship-building skills can break down.

Finding ways to remain connected, empathetic, and inclusive to those who hurt or disappoint us is incredibly difficult, but this is where the heart of our work lives. Traditionally we have no problem addressing conflict in one way: we punish students, come down hard on them, lecture them, and let them know just how much they have disappointed us. Of course, this rarely changes the behavior, and the message that kids internalize often at quite an early age in elementary or middle school is, "I don't belong here," "School isn't for me," "I'm a bad kid." This is the root of the school-to-prison pipeline, not to mention where a lot of implicit bias can rear its ugly head and lead to disproportionate and unfair discipline. As a country we have a lot of work to do to repair this messaging.

Let's be extremely clear. RJ is *not* about a removal of consequences, permitting misbehavior, or stripping school staff of their safety or their ability to do their jobs. RJ as a philosophy, like every educator, is absolutely in support of (logical) consequences for harmful behavior, absolutely about supporting teachers and administration (and student) safety, and we want nothing more than to promote a healthy learning and work environment for all. So, it is a comfort to know that we are actually all on the same page, setting clear expectations and upholding them, although the route to this success may look quite different depending on the approach—restorative or retributive justice.

We have stated that RJ is about creating relationships, even and especially in times of conflict. And look, we must all understand that relationships are hard. Who amongst us has not struggled with our partners, friends, or family members? It's not easy to show love and caring *while* you are being hurt or disappointed by someone. This shift in mindset is incredibly hard, and yet incredibly simple. Just think of this messaging:

> What you did was harmful to yourself and others. It was unacceptable and will not be tolerated in this school AND we still want you here. We value you, and we believe in your success. We want to help you make better choices, repair what has happened, and to learn from this experience.

It is this "AND" that is extremely important. When you do not make this "AND" clear with words and actions, when you leave that "we still want you here" part out, students will receive a totally different "AND" in their heads, something like, "...AND we don't want you here AND we don't like you AND we don't believe in you."

This is the true cause of many students dropping out or repeating harmful behavior.

It is very human to want the person who is hurting you, or who you are watching hurt others, to disappear. That would be easier. And yet, most educators are in fact deeply dedicated to supporting all students, even the most difficult, with a passion rarely seen in other professions. And so we are all looking for ways to help those students. Another quote that we often remind ourselves of during those hard times is, "Those who are hardest to love usually need it the most," but this is incredibly difficult. Often the other pressures educators feel—standardized tests, evaluations, large class sizes, etc.—leave little room for expanded empathy and intervention for students causing harm to the school community. Teachers are already carrying many great loads.

But we, as a society, are committed to all students, and in public school settings we are mandated to educate all students, and we know the costs to society of pushing students out. So we dig in, we find ways to give even more, and relationships is where we start, because it is the number one key to changing behaviors and increasing success for all.

Different categories of relationship (and all of them are important!)

Research[2] has shown that having even one type of relationship in school can greatly help a student show up and persist.

These relationships fall into three important categories:

- Having a trusted adult in the building (anyone from the principal to a coach to cafeteria staff, someone who has shown an interest in and care for the student).

- A healthy connection with a peer.

- Strong investment in the school (often called "school bonding"), which can result from the school offering valuable activities such as sports or music or art programs that the student enjoys.

When a young person (or indeed anyone) causes harm, we need to nurture these three relationships. A good circle conference will often have members from each represented—a trusted adult, a peer (or peers) who cares about the student, and a member of the school administration who cares about that student's success should all be invited. It takes everyone sitting in a circle conference with the same message—"What you did was hurtful AND we still want you here." Not just the words, though, but also the actions that back them up.

The word *relationship* is funny, because our connections can vary immensely in depth and quality. Think of someone who asks you, "How are you doing?" to which you respond, "I'm fine thanks,

---

2   Roehlkepartain, E. C., Pekel, K., Syvertsen, A. K., Sethi, J., Sullivan, T. K. and Scales, P. C. (2017) *Relationships First: Creating Connections that Help Young People Thrive.* Minneapolis, MN: Search Institute. CDC (Centers for Disease Control and Prevention) (2009) *School Connectedness: Strategies for Increasing Protective Factors among Youth.* Atlanta, GA: US Department of Health and Human Services. Available at: www.cdc.gov/healthyyouth/protective/pdf/connectedness.pdf; Blum, R. (2005) *School Connectedness: Improving the Lives of Students.* Baltimore, MD: Johns Hopkins Bloomberg School of Public Health; National Research Council and Institute of Medicine (2004) *Engaging Schools: Fostering High School Students' Motivation to Learn.* Washington, DC: The National Academies Press.

and you?" This could be a response to a random co-worker or casual acquaintance. Now think of someone who might ask you the same question but where you pause, take a deep breath, and actually start describing your mother's recent health issues and how worried you are about her, or how you have been struggling to decide about changing careers, or any other significant thing that is actually going on in your life. This second type of person is more likely to be a close friend or family member, someone you have grown close to through many positive interactions. To get a student to open up, or to take accountability, or to admit being wrong and to apologize, or to honestly explain themselves, requires that second type of person being at the table for them. If you have an "I'm fine, thanks" type of relationship with this student, how can we expect them to be vulnerable and honest in a circle with you? When you look at it this way, it's actually amazing how well some RJ circles go, how brave and honest and accountable students can be with adults of authority they barely know.

In addition to the three relationship categories mentioned above, it is extremely important to note a fourth category: relationship with self. This plays an outsized role with many of our young people. Not only do they need to feel good about their school, peers, and teachers to feel part of the community and find success; they also need to feel good about themselves. And how many of our students struggle with this? How can they feel connected if they don't feel worthy? How can they be asked to repair harm if they feel incapable? Many young people (and adults) bully themselves in their own mind and carry immense shame and a general lack of confidence. This will surely inhibit their ability to create and maintain positive connections with others.

And so our community-building activities and circles must also include ways to help young people learn about themselves, their strengths and positive qualities, appreciate their journey and their culture, and show themselves compassion for their failings. This can be achieved through autobiographical writing, "Who am I?" projects, or what we like to call JOY projects—self-directed work of the student's choice that highlights something they feel good about. There are a million ways to help young people build their positive sense of self. We could write a whole book (and yes, one will be coming!) about these activities to build community with others and with self, and this work is essential.

Let's realize that *relationship* is really just a proxy for *trust*. Think on that for a moment. Without trust we cannot be speaking about relationships or about being vulnerable and accountable as a community. When we ask students to open up in a circle, we are asking for their trust, trust that we will use the information to help them, not to cause further harm, that we will be confidential and respectful. When we ask adults to take accountability for failures, we can only do so successfully in a space where they feel safe to be imperfect, and receive support and coaching rather than shame and blame or consequences for their career. And just like relationships, building and maintaining trust is also incredibly difficult, especially for students or adults who have experienced trauma or in other ways had their ability to trust severely impaired. You may hear that communication is the number one key to good relationships, and there is some truth to this, but really it is communication *with* trust that makes us successful in a relationship with others. Often our communication is not perfect, but when you trust the person speaking to you, you are willing to take their lead and follow them through the storm.

Nicholas remembers a story where he saw this power of relationships to be true.

While working with young people in Vermont, he was able to plan a week-long summer hiking trip. Without really knowing much about what they had signed up for, a handful of 5th and 6th grade boys showed up to embark on this adventure. It was a tough trail, with hours of hiking each day. The trip was a success, difficult, but rewarding. Nicholas always remembers this summer in awe that these young people were willing to follow him for a week on a grueling hike—not because they wanted to tackle these mountain trails (most had never really hiked before), but because they knew and trusted Nicholas as an adult and as an educator. The relationship is what had them sign up and put their faith in the trip.

David has seen a profound shift when teachers view challenging students through the lens of relationships. When working as a dean in the Bronx, he remembers getting a referral from a teacher that a 9th grade boy was often walking around the class, disrupting the lessons, and had even called her racist. He met with the student and the teacher individually, to discuss, and then set up mediation. David was impressed how the teacher, in their pre-conference meeting, had not focused as much on the rules that the student was breaking or how he was being disruptive, but instead kept talking about how she liked him and wanted to find a way for him to be more successful in the class. She wanted to have a better relationship with him, in spite of, or especially because he had claimed she didn't like him because of his race. This type of accusation would make a lot of educators pull away in discomfort, but she wanted to sit down and talk things through, to let him know where she was coming from.

During the lunchtime mediation, the student started out upset and defensive: "She's always picking on me, telling me to get back in my seat and calling out my name in front of everyone. I think she doesn't like me; it's because I'm black." I asked him why he felt that race was an issue. "I'm loud and I like to move around a lot, that's how black people are; she's a quiet white lady so she just doesn't get it." I asked the teacher how she felt about what was happening in the class. She responded by saying that she liked him, that she liked his energy and passion, but that when he was walking around all the time it was very distracting and hard for other students to focus. It had nothing to do with the color of his skin, just that she wanted him to get the lessons.

This is where things could have easily stalled, or she could have simply demanded he follow the rules, but amazingly, she started to think around how she could accommodate the needs she was hearing him express. "I hear that you have trouble staying in one place, but when you leave your work on your desk to walk around, you miss a lot of the notes. I just need you to not be disruptive in the middle of a lesson, as you move a little. I know it can be a difficult class, but you are good at math and can pass if you put in a little more effort this semester. What if I got you a clipboard?" she offered, "so when you are feeling restless, you could carry your notes to an empty desk, move a little, and then keep taking notes," she offered. Usually a tough kid, even David was surprised when the student responded, "You would do that for me?" Rather than trying to deny being racist and enforce the rules, she had shown that she was only focusing on his best interests, that she wanted him in the class, and that she cared most about him as a person. He was clearly touched on some level. "Okay, let's try that," he said.

She did end up giving him a clipboard the next class. Some days it really worked, and others she still struggled with his behavior in class, but the claims of racism evaporated and their relationship was clearly better, and the class was more productive and peaceful as a whole. He asked her for help more, and he was generally more respectful to her in front of the class. Rather than threatening punishment in the mediation, she had focused on improving their relationship, on his needs while expressing her own, and that was more effective at producing results than any punishment would have been in the situation.

So let's clarify. We use the term "restorative justice" as an umbrella term that refers to a system that is equitable and fair, and that utilizes relationships to achieve success and repair harm in times of conflict. "Restorative practices" are all of those activities that help grow, nurture, and maintain those positive relationships. We are actually practicing how to be in relationship with each other, how to share and take accountability. And it truly is about *practice.* These trusted relationships are earned. There really aren't any shortcuts here.

Practice is all about consistency
Dr. Brené Brown, quoting Dr. John Gottman,[3] said that it is not one overt act that creates strong relationships. You can make a

---

3 Gottman, J. (2011) "John Gottman on trust and betrayal." *Greater Good Magazine*, October 29. Available at: https://greatergood.berkeley.edu/article/item/john_gottman_on_trust_and_betrayal

grand marriage proposal, with flowers and violins and a helicopter ride over the city. And this may even get you a YES! But this marriage will not last without the daily commitment to honest communication and each other's support. In the same way, we *earn* relationships with students and other staff by showing up for them, physically, emotionally, and consistently, as well as by admitting our failures and repairing harm when it occurs. Often young people will come to you with a deep lack of trust in their parents, peers, teachers, the police, and society as a whole, and many of them with good reason. It is our daily grind of showing that we deserve their trust that will help them move forward in their social and emotional learning (SEL).

Having systems in place that appear restorative but end up disappointing or harming the student deepen the mistrust and disconnection. Asking resistant students to immediately be trusting after an intense event occurs just won't work, but small, safe, community-building circles will slowly earn their trust that they can be open and unguarded in the community. Often answering prompts as simple as, "What is your favorite food?" or "What is something you enjoy doing outside of school?" when facilitated correctly and with safety can be much needed practice for these students on how to open up and trust that their community will respect them when they decide to share of themselves. This, as well as practicing accountability in a space where everyone takes responsibility for something, can be a hugely positive experience for rewiring the brain and opening the heart to what it is to be open and part of a community. Many students who commit harm are asked to think about what they could have done differently in an instance of conflict, but rarely do they get to experience the teacher or other students also thinking about what they could have done differently. We often do an exercise when training school staff, demonstrating an accountability circle, (discussed in depth in Chapter 10) where we ask each adult to own something that they have done to contribute to a failure occurring at their school. In this type of accountability circle, all members are encouraged to practice accountability, and imagine what they might do differently to make the situation better.

This is not just the person who is seen as responsible for addressing the particular issue, or simply the person that might be seen as "at fault"; we ask that everyone flex their own accountability muscles.

This is also probably a great place to point out something that should be obvious, but rarely is—if these practices are not occurring among staff members, but you are expecting that it be done with (or to) students, you are missing something hugely important. If you believe in this work for students, why not for staff members as well? If you don't feel it is useful for yourself, then why spend time on it with students? Strong relationships between staff are as important as between staff and students, and the benefits will show up as well. Often this is achieved during professional development time, where community-building circles or other bonding activities can occur. Conflict between staff can also be handled either in the traditional manner—a discipline meeting discussing the rules or values broken—or it can be framed in terms of school relationships that have been harmed and how to empower all parties to repair the harm and move forward.

When we get the common question of, "Why is this student not responding to my restorative approach?" it should be clear that you might not yet have the relationship needed at this point. And this may not be any fault of your own; it is difficult and takes time to develop these bonds, especially with many of the time, space, and mandated demands that schools have. Not to mention that we must remember it is so incredibly hard to take responsibility for your actions, and to be vulnerable, to share, to show flaws as humans...especially without strong and trusted relationships. It is hard even for invested adults. We don't always make the connection between how difficult it is for us to make an apology or admit fault, while we expect the world from some of our youth in this regard.

We often do an exercise when training school staff, where we do an accountability circle, and ask each adult to own something that they have done to contribute to a failure occurring at their school. This activity is often quite challenging for many. No one wants to show flaws or state where they have let others or themselves down, especially if they feel that others were more at fault than themselves! We want to look good and feel good! But this activity is a great reminder of what we ask students to do in restorative circles, often when looking directly into the eyes of disappointed family members, upset staff, or students they have harmed. No easy task! Of course this is always easier with school staff who have already put in the work and practice of building community. When teachers know each other well, when administration has created a safe space for learning from mistakes (and shown the ability to admit their own!), these folks feel more open about being vulnerable. The hard work is a lot easier. The same goes for students—practice accountability, and the work will pay dividends.

And so we spend time as a school and staff building community and relationships. And when a harm occurs, we spend time conferencing and pre-conferencing to prepare for a circle so that it is more likely to be successful. And this is the truth about RJ— that we know it won't always be perfect, but we believe it will be *more likely to succeed*, to change negative behaviors, increase attendance, respect, and academic success, and mitigate implicit bias. We know that traditional discipline is not working, and can have devastating negative consequences. And so we work to shift to a restorative mindset that has been shown (albeit not every time) on so many occasions to produce positive results. We sit in conflict AND remain unwavering in our commitment to keeping students in school in a safe and productive way. We humble ourselves as educators and examine our own actions as well as our students'. Maybe the way we raised our voice at that student, or our sarcastic comment, might have contributed to the conflict that happened that day. And that does not excuse their behavior, but we can also own our own behavior and work to repair our relationship, because, after all, we still work together come Monday. And that Monday can either be one where two community members who worked out their problems and shook hands start afresh, or where a student who was removed by security and was suspended will simply walk back into class without us knowing what will happen next or how they feel. I know that the second scenario sounds much more stressful to me as a teacher!

But how can we "do" restorative justice? We're not restorative justice professionals!

A common push-back on all restorative work will come from teachers and staff who (rightly!) claim, "Hey, I've never been trained in this stuff. I'm a Math teacher, what do I know about running circles and community building?" Absolutely! That's exactly why, by having these activities occur regularly (as time will allow) amongst staff, they can get practice in circles and such activities and a chance to see that much of this work is simple, fun, and very do-able for anyone. What can seem like an intimidating philosophy will quickly be seen as something often as simple as sitting in a circle, passing a talking piece, and answering simple questions about ourselves, our thoughts, or our feelings. Not so scary after you have done it a few times in a safe space.

And, of course, the opposite is also completely true. Running a circle or participating in one can actually be quite challenging and sometimes scary. It will not always feel fun and do-able. We have facilitated circles with school staff where we ask questions like, "What got you into education?" and then we build towards more vulnerable questions like, "What was hard for you during middle or high school?" Often we will get two types of responses, comments like, "That was really fun, we don't often get to spend time as a staff simply sharing about ourselves." And this is the same thing many students experience. But we will also hear, "That was actually really difficult, sharing those tough memories from when I was young was hard in front of all these people I work with everyday." And this is also what students experience—it can be extremely difficult and at times painful to open up like this. This is a pertinent reminder to us, as facilitators, to stop for a moment and recognize just what it is that we are asking of students, a radical shift in how they have learned to act and behave in school with their peers and teachers. Often it's a great deal of fun, but it can also be scary and difficult. We need to keep up these practices as constant reminders not to shift into autopilot. And these reminders are not just needed for circles. You may be a math teacher asking a student to "solve for X," up at the whiteboard in front of the class, and we must remember that it can be an intense, emotional experience to have to say, "I don't know how to do it, I'm confused." Almost none of us are good at practicing being uncomfortable while remaining connected. This comes down to spending time connecting to each other in meaningful ways—via relationships.

"If I know who you are, I am more likely to trust you, I am more likely to respect the ways in which we are different"—this goes a long way in schools. Students are much less likely to bully each other when they spend time getting to know each other. This also extends into issues of race, class, and culture. Knowing each other and finding connections can often dispel the sense of "otherness" that can occur, causing fear and even aggression. You may see a simple circle question of, "What do you like to do with your free time?" result in students from diverse backgrounds instantly connecting over a love of video games or skateboarding or a local sports team. Suddenly they are looking at each other and seeing something in common. "If I don't know about your experience in life, I need to learn about it or I cannot connect." "If I didn't grow up Jewish, or transgender, or as an immigrant, or as wealthy and privileged, I cannot connect and trust you." It is only through creating a safe space for sharing life experiences that we can begin to understand each other and trust. "What does it mean to be Jewish, Christian, or Muslim in America?" "What does it mean to be gay or lesbian in this school?" These types of questions, when you slowly and carefully build up to them, can open up whole new levels of trust and connectedness between students (and adults) of diverse backgrounds.

We all know that conflict can lead to total disaster—an argument with a co-worker that makes you wish you could work at another school, or even a romantic relationship that ended so badly you wished you could move to a new city. Most of us have experienced conflict as a negative occurrence and would do anything to avoid it.

Conflict isn't all bad...

But what if conflict could actually result in *better* relationships? This isn't as crazy as it might sound. Think of going on a road trip with a romantic partner. Travelling can be hard and stressful; maybe you even have a big fight at a gas station that has you storming off in anger. But when you stay committed to that love and to that relationship, you are able to argue, make up, learn from the experience, and grow. In the end, that difficult road trip might bring you closer together as a couple.

It is often when we experience something difficult, if we don't walk away but stay present in that conflict, that we can grow incredibly close. In fact, with a lot of young people, if you ask, some of their best friends are people they previously disliked or even fought with. If you walk through the flames together, sometimes you will emerge bonded by that experience. And that is one of the *promises*, the exciting aspects of RJ, that through learning to engage in conflict in healthy ways, we will grow stronger and closer as a community. This is a radical and exciting shift in mindset, one that takes a new skillset in how to navigate conflict, to grow more comfortable with it.

Ultimately, we build relationships and trust over time with our actions. At one school, we developed an RJ office where we mediated a lot of conflict, supported and coached students who were struggling with negative behaviors, had meetings with families, etc. At first, students saw this through the lens that they already possessed: that it was simply the dean's office, a place you got sent when you were in trouble. But slowly we were able to show them that it was much more than that. Yes, it was a place where students might spend time in conferences and meetings after they had caused a harm. But it was also a place where we did check-ins with students, learned more about what they were going through at home, gave them a bite to snack on when they were hungry, and mediated fights before they happened because we were tipped off to them ahead of time. People would share this type of information with us because we demonstrated that we wanted to prevent harm, not just punish the students who caused it. We showed that we cared about their personal circumstances, connecting them with helpful resources, that we would listen without judgment, and where students were often asked to speak with other students to think creatively about solutions. We showed that traditional discipline was a last resort rather than an automatic go-to.

Often you think of the most problematic students having the worst relationships with school staff, after day-in, day-out conflicts. We had the opposite—the "high flyers," those students referred frequently to our office. They almost became interns in the RJ office. Sometimes they would pop their head in uninvited to say, "Hey, is that the freshman who got into a fight today? Can I talk to him about my freshman year, when I was buck wild? I want to share some words with him." Sometimes we would formally facilitate this, an older student sharing what they had been through and how it had turned out. These were powerful meetings. Probably the greatest success for our office was one day when a female student burst into our office one morning to yell in anger, "Yo, we need to have one of those circle things right now or I'm about to fight this girl. She's talking crazy!" This speaks volumes. First, this was a student who had fought several times previously, and now the social and emotional learning had occurred to allow her to pause before immediately giving into her rage. It also showed that she trusted us, that she had faith in what we could do to help her, that she could be open about being in conflict, that she was allowed to have her anger but wanted to do something different with it rather than fight and hurt her education. She had faith that the circle would work, and that we had faith in her, to have that conversation safely in our space. This was a moment where you could see the power of relationships, not just when times were good and the student was happy, like when she just got her first job and wanted to come share the news, but rather at a time when the chips were down, when conflict was hot, and when only her gut instinct on who to trust had kicked in.

BUILDING PYRAMIDS

When Emilio first walked into our offices, he looked disheveled. He shuffled through the door wearing sagging pants and an oversized t-shirt. He was standoffish, barely answering basic questions, and not making eye contact, and I immediately caught the smell of weed as he placed his jacket down on a chair next to mine.

Due to his gang involvement, by the age of 19 Emilio had had countless run-ins with the law and had experienced a range of negative consequences. His probation officer (PO) had reached out to my organization as a last resort, because I work at a community justice program in Harlem that has been effective with other challenging cases in the past.

Emilio's work with us was basically an ultimatum—either he engage in our program or he faced going back to jail. So this was somewhere between being mandated and a choice. To Emilio, this was the lesser of two evils, so here he was.

I believe in meeting young people where they are, and then helping them move gradually from where they are at the moment to where it is that they would like to go in the future, even if they don't have a clear understanding of how to get there yet. This approach makes sense to a lot of youth; it's like having a road map that is tailored to their needs. To me, this is the core of the restorative approach. The way I say it to young people is that my role is like a taxi cab driver. It's not the cab driver's responsibility to choose the destination; the passenger picks that. My job is to help get the passenger there safely, choosing from the best routes available.

First, it's all about building rapport, and that is how I approached our work with Emilio. I spent that first intake meeting trying to get him to see that we were not there to be punitive; we were trying to look towards his future. His family was exhausted, and ready to give up. His mother had reported that his younger brother had begun modeling some of Emilio's dangerous behaviors. So I asked him straight up, "Everybody says you're trying to throw your life away, that you almost want to go back to jail. Is that how it is from your perspective?" After a pause, Emilio looked at me for the first time and said, "No, but nobody helps me when I'm trying. So, if they don't care, then I don't care." I took that statement in and nodded before asking, "Okay, if I was to commit to assisting you, one piece at a time, like, if I help you achieve some of your short-term goals, would you be open to working on some longer-term goals?"

I took some more time asking questions, getting to know Emilio's motivations and worldview. I asked him what it was that he really wanted. As it turned out, he really wanted to learn a vocation and make money to be helpful to his family. In fact, even his criminal activities, in his mind, were an attempt to put money in his pocket that he could then use to help his family. He felt an immense responsibility as the eldest child in a single-parent household.

At the end of that first meeting we laid out a few small and achievable goals, such as attending weekly meetings to work on his resume and to participate in group discussion circles. Unfortunately, almost immediately, he began to miss those appointments or was late and disengaged. We are required to give a full report on the participants, and based on his absences, I got a phone call from his PO, who was at the point of having to pull him from the program and hold him accountable for not attending.

This work is rarely straightforward or without setbacks. So I asked the PO to give us one more shot at getting through to him. We hadn't yet had a chance to do a home visit and talk with him one more time. "If that's not effective, then so be it," was my plea. I wasn't ready to give up on Emilio just yet. Members of my team made the home visit with Emilio's mother, explaining the things we were putting in place to support him. They asked her if she could try to reinforce this work at home. They acknowledged the difficulty of this, after her years of frustration, but stressed that we still believed in moving him forward. And luckily, little by little, with this group effort, things began to turn around for Emilio.

First, he started meeting the goal of being at appointments on time. Then, he began to step up and go above and beyond his assignments. Not only did he make his cover letter and resume, he actually went online by himself to research different ways to format these documents and represent himself in the best way possible. I looked into specialty programs that would allow him to enter into the construction trades, but I found out that he would need to be involved in an academic program to earn his high school equivalency (HSE), as he had previously dropped out of high school. Showing him that I was invested in him succeeding, without judgment, this really encouraged him, and before I could even get the paperwork together, he had already travelled on his own to enroll in a program to earn his HSE.

Emilio began to think about and plan for his future. I am happy to say that he is now only four weeks from earning his HSE diploma and six weeks from beginning his training in welding. He is very proud of where he is at. Several factors helped in this journey. He earned a stipend through his HSE program, so he was still able to fulfill his goal of helping out his family. It also helped that he was the one who found this particular program, even though I was there to provide resources and ideas. I was there to give him some direction, but ultimately, he was the one to make the call and sign himself up for this program, which was important to his feeling of worth and personal investment.

As I mentioned, a huge part of our program's success has been a result of our commitment to building rapport, and developing strong relationships. I can remember a trip our group took to the Museum of Natural History. Emilio still wasn't that open with the other young people, so he kind of hung by my side a bit. At one point the two of us were standing in front of a massive exhibit on ancient pyramids. We were both surprised to learn that pyramids originated in South America and not in Egypt. I remember Emilio turning to me to say, "See, construction is the best occupation you can be in! There's always been construction for the whole history of the world. You always need people to build things. That's why I want to be in construction." And that just blew me away, that he made a personal connection between the exhibit and his own aspirations. It also really showed me that he was serious about learning a trade. It's these brief but deeply personal moments that help build trust and connection.

I recently spoke with Emilio's mother to say that the encouragement we had all been giving him had really started to pay off. She agreed, and added that his younger brother, the one she had been so concerned about imitating Emilio, was now actually being influenced positively by him. Emilio had been talking with him about his own choices and mistakes, what it was really like out on the streets. He had even started helping his little brother do his homework in the evenings. Hearing the relief in his mother's voice was thrilling.

Emilio's progression was not linear or without obstacles, however. It was slow and difficult work at times. Even when he first attended our group meetings, he was often there, but not engaged, staring off, not wanting to participate. But eventually, as his life came together and he saw some tangible results, he began to give back more to others in the program.

One afternoon, a new young man joined Emilio's group discussion. There were 10 of us in the circle. Some were there voluntarily, some mandated. And here was this new participant, standoffish, like Emilio used to be. When it came to this new person, he expressed that, "Yeah, I'm gonna be here as long as it takes to get through this program for my PO. But that's it. As long as I'm here when I'm supposed to be here, I don't really have to be involved. I'm not knocking myself out with this thing." He clearly wanted to let the group know that he was just going through the motions, that he couldn't care less. And I remember Emilio speaking right to him, without hesitation, saying, "Yeah, that's one way to go about it, because I came into this with the same mindset. If you waste the opportunity while you're here, that will be your choice. But if you actually give these people a chance, they can help you move your whole situation forward." Then he shared his story, how he had started out in the same way but was now on his way to "doing A, B,

C, and D," and how he now felt like he was moving in a whole other direction than he had been when he first came in through that door.

And that's the thing, a lot of young people will really hear advice more clearly when it is coming peer-to-peer, from someone they can relate to. This insight from Emilio was much more effective than anything I could say to them. I could see that this new young man was really hearing Emilio, taking him seriously, more so than when I was speaking to him. And you could feel Emilio start to recognize the power that he was now holding, to transform himself and others around him, and I know he enjoys being a leader and a role model in this way.

It comes down to treating people like people. Believing in people. Allowing them to be the main force in finding their own solutions. I simply kept my word to help Emilio get where he said he wanted to go, to listen, and to do my best to drive the taxi.

Keyonn, New York

Story debrief

Although this story deals with a young man outside of a traditional school setting, the lessons still ring true. Keyonn immediately got to work getting to know Emilio, building empathy and demonstrating his support. He worked to make him feel welcome in the program, despite his past choices. He set realistic expectations and communicated them clearly. Ultimately he presented himself as more of a *coach* than a *cop*, someone more concerned with his success than just seeking his compliance. What we love about the ending of this story is how the strong relationship paid dividends to the community, one of the most exciting results of a strong RJ ecosystem. Emilio ended up acting as a mentor to a younger member of the group during the circle conversation, and his words had power. This was a benefit to the young man hearing from him as a peer, and also helped to improve Emilio's sense of worth and agency as a community member, something he was previously seeking from gangs and other negative settings. We have seen this countless times in schools. A student who ends up in the RJ office slowly begins to develop better SEL and conflict skills, and will eventually mature and progress, often stopping in the office and wanting to talk to younger students who have got into trouble. They love to share how they "used to act like that," fighting or skipping school or using drugs, and how they had moved on from that behavior and were doing much better now in life. Students will listen to them with rapt attention the way they will not listen to an adult they perceive as giving them yet another lecture. We can see from this story how one strong relationship can help a young person progress, but it can also help other relationships start to form, as young people feel empowered to act as mentors to others.

2

The Five Pillars of Restorative Justice

CORE GUIDING PRINCIPLES

So what *exactly* is restorative justice? To be honest, there are countless credible definitions and some debate over the meaning of the term, even amongst professional practitioners. The definition that we, at the NC4RJ, prefer to use is, "A relational approach to conflict and harm." For us it is as simple as that, focusing on building and maintaining strong relationships as we navigate conflict and harm. We also like to add that RJ answers the question: "How do we provide the space for accountability and build relationships at the same time?"

Some other definitions of RJ include:

Restorative justice is a process to involve, to the extent possible, those who have a stake in a specific offense and to collectively identify and address harms, needs and obligations, in order to heal and put things right as possible.[1]

Restorative justice is a way of seeing crime as more than breaking the law—it also causes harm to people, relationships, and the community. So a just response must address those harms as well.

---

1   Zehr, H. with Gohar, A. (2002) *The Little Book of Restorative Justice* (p.37). Intercourse, PA: Good Books.

If they are willing, the best way to do this is for the parties themselves to meet to discuss the harms and how to bring about resolution. (Other approaches are available if they are unable or unwilling to meet.) Sometimes those meetings lead to transformational changes in their lives.[2]

"Restorative justice" means practices, policies, and programs informed by and sensitive to the needs of crime victims that are designed to encourage offenders to accept responsibility for repairing the harm caused by their offense by providing safe and supportive opportunities for voluntary participation and communication between the victim, the offender, their families, and relevant community members.[3]

Restorative Justice is a community response to crime and other misconduct that focuses on addressing the harms done to victims and communities by holding offenders meaningfully accountable for their offenses.[4]

The goal of Restorative Justice is the creation of safe, healthy communities. Such communities are created when there are opportunities for victims to have their needs addressed and when offenders are integrated into the community as positive, contributing citizens.[5]

We don't believe it is worth the time to debate the perfect definition of RJ here, or to argue the differences between restorative justice and restorative practices as we see them. In fact, we often encourage folks to explore the many definitions of RJ, such as those mentioned above, and to find the one that best resonates with their goals, experiences, and needs, or to create their own definition after doing this work for some time.

---

2   International Institute of Restorative Practices, see www.justicereparatrice. org/www.restorativejustice.org/university-classroom/01introduction/ tutorial-introduction-to-restorative-justice/lesson-1-definition/lesson-1-definition

3   Washington State Legislature, RCW 13.40.020, 'Definitions' (27). Available at: https://app.leg.wa.gov/rcw/default.aspx?cite=13.40.020

4   Restorative Justice Coalition of Oregon, see http://rjoregon.org/what-is-rj

5   www.ncjrs.gov/pdffiles1/nij/248890.pdf

What we find far more useful is to explore some of the key elements of RJ philosophy, the five pillars, as we will call them. These combine to build a powerful lens that we can use to analyze current or proposed systems. We find it can be helpful when evaluating a proposed policy or potential action to look at these five pillars and see how well this action or decision would serve them. They make up the foundation of the restorative ecosystem and clearly explain what it is we are out to achieve They are aspirational, meaning that you may not be able to completely fulfill each of them with every action you take with your students and staff, but they should serve as a guiding light when working to bring about a restorative system to your community.

The five pillars of restorative justice

- Acknowledge and confront conflict.

- Engage all stakeholders.

- Empower the author[6] and the victim.

- Value empathy.

- Develop agency.

Let's take a look at each in turn, a little more closely.

Conflict happens and being conflict aware
Teach young people and adults to engage with conflict in a healthy and sustainable manner.

We have dedicated an entire chapter to this topic of conflict (see

---

6   When we use the term "author," we are referring to the author of an act who has caused harm, the person whose actions have negatively impacted members of the community and/or themselves. This term is chosen to separate the act from the person who authored it, as well as re-enforcing the idea that we are each empowered in our decision-making to impact our community.

Chapter 3), but it's worth touching on some key points here as well. It would seem that the traditional form of school discipline and the criminal justice system strive to eliminate conflict altogether—if you could just suspend enough times and give out enough detentions, students would never fight again. Or if we could just keep raising the prison sentences and get tough enough on crime, no one would ever sell or abuse drugs. Unfortunately these attempts have never worked. Young people and adults are humans, and it is only natural that tempers will flare and arguments will happen. And most criminal activity is a result of many more factors—poverty, addiction, mental health issues, lack of community resources, etc.—these factors do not change despite harsh prison sentences. In fact, anytime you have people together, conflict will arise. The sooner we accept this reality, that conflict is normal, the sooner we can move away from shame and blame and come from a place of acceptance and a willingness to better deal with conflicts. We are not, of course, condoning fights or drug use in school, and we truly believe that a lot of conflict can and should be deterred and avoided, but totally eliminating it is a fool's errand. As long as conflict exists, our students (and our staff) need to know how to work through it, to have difficult conversations, and to grow their skills in repairing harmed relationships while remaining inclusive to those who have caused harm.

And what a relief that is to know, that conflict is totally normal and can never be totally avoided! Think of being a dean in a new school. If you see your job as preventing conflict, then the first time students get into an argument in the hallway you might feel like you have failed. And feeling like a failure is never a good place to start making positive change. But if you have a restorative mindset, and you build restorative systems, when a conflict arises you will think, "Okay, here is the first conflict. We have been preparing for this; our staff and students have practiced the language and skills they need to work through it. Now let's get to work and hopefully we can all emerge stronger as a community after working through it."

Nicholas likes to relate this to personal relationships. Someone with little life experience may think that a great relationship is one with no conflict at all, but for most of us, we know that all couples (and friends) have arguments and disagreements. If you immediately run away when you have any conflict, you will not be in any relationship for very long! Relationships should not be overwhelmed by conflict, but knowing how to communicate and remain loving when times get tough is the true work of any solid and authentic relationship. And it's hard! It's hard to own up to our mistakes, to be honest, to have difficult conversations, to advocate for what we need, to know what we want. We need to respect just how difficult this is for adults, let alone younger students. But this is the work of any strong and long-lasting relationship. So, rather than fearing conflict, let's try to prepare for it, maintain our principles and missions, and teach our youth how to better deal with conflict around and within them. After all, in many cases, when two or more people work through a very tough situation in the right way, the experience can actually bond them and bring them closer together. This is the true promise and power of RJ, that conflict can actually bring us closer together rather than tear us apart.

Engage all stakeholders

Everyone who has an interest in the conflict is welcomed to the process.

This principle, again, runs counter-intuitive to many existing discipline systems—in schools and in courts, rarely do the affected parties meet to make their voices heard and to collectively find solutions and resolutions. What we mean is that anyone who has an interest in this conflict is welcome at the circle, or conference, or whatever action is being taken to address the situation. Of course we need to make careful decisions about who is there and when, and to match the severity of the harm to the amount of people attending. But teachers, parents, and other students are rarely consulted in the current forms of school discipline. This is the traditional state of affairs in most schools where discipline is primarily doled out by school administration or by state guidelines, to the student or students who are presumed to have broken the rules. Many times a teacher sends a student to the office and they just don't know what happens after that, especially if you don't have the time to hunt down administration and ask for details. Before you know it the student may return to your classroom amid a great deal of confusion and unresolved conflict. This is a recipe for disaster, and often results in a breakdown of relationships, if not further incidents occurring.

Think of what it looks like to expand stakeholder involvement and fulfill this RJ principle. We can all imagine a situation of traditional discipline where two students were seen arguing in the hallway and one student shoves the other. The student who did the shoving is pulled into the office and given a punishment. This is an extremely narrow view of resolving the conflict. It does not take into account the context of the argument, the actions of the student who was shoved, or the impact on the community. The punishment (detention, cafeteria duty, etc.) may deter the behavior and we may never have another incident like this, but more likely we can easily see how this punishment may do nothing to prevent further conflict. The student may have been punished in this way many times in the past, may have given up caring if he gets punished, and the reason for the argument between the two students may remain, ensuring that things could get physical again. The student may also feel an injustice over the punishment. Perhaps he was pushed first, but that previous action was not seen, or he felt that he was disrespected in some way, or may even have been bullied by the person he shoved—all issues that would need to be unpacked, but probably would not be if he was just sent to an administrator for punishment. In systems like this, students will not avoid conflict but simply hide them better, finding more secretive places to fight, such as bathrooms or nearby off-campus locations. This is not the result we are after, even if it means fewer disturbances in the school hallway.

Now, imagine a conference or circle with the two students seen fighting, teachers who care about them, other students who have an insight into the argument, and perhaps parents or other concerned parties. The full context can be discovered, accountability can be taken for different aspects of the conflict, and meaningful solutions and consequences can be agreed on. Of course, time and resources need to be dedicated to this process, which is no easy task, but we can all see how this way of addressing the conflict would be infinitely more successful at preventing future conflict than simply giving a detention to the student who did the shoving. This is not to say that there will be no consequence to this act of aggression; certainly we are not advocating for this behavior to be overlooked. But with all stakeholders at the table a more logical, impactful, and deterring consequence can be agreed on. RJ is not about abandoning consequences; it is about better consequences.

Involving stakeholders in mediating conflict is also a *huge* opportunity for SEL. One of the best things a student can learn in this regard is the concept of *impact*, or how their actions affect their own lives and the lives of others. This is a way to build empathy and develop agency. Take the example of two students fighting in a hallway, as mentioned above. Many times students are asked after such an incident, "Who do you think was affected or impacted by your behavior in the hallway?" And countless times we hear the same thing in response: either "I don't know," or that it only affected themselves (because they got into trouble) and the other student (because they got pushed or hurt, for instance). This illustrates perfectly the extent to which many young people are able to view impact without proper coaching and teaching. Their responses make sense to them, and yet, being able to go wider in their view of impact will profoundly affect their growth as accountable individuals and members of the community. This seems so obvious to many adults, that their actions have affected many others, but most young people have not had the opportunity to reflect on impact, and, depending on their age, may even be lacking in full development of the parts of the brain that would allow them to fully process the effect they are having on others.

It is fascinating to meet with a young person who believes they have only affected themselves or maybe one other person in such cases as the hallway argument, and to then have stakeholders at a table or circle share how they were affected for the student to hear. One by one, the student listens. Maybe a teacher shares how their whole class rushed to the door to watch the fight and their lesson was thrown off track that day. Maybe a parent explains that they had to use a sick day to leave work and come down to the school to pick up their child. Maybe a younger student explains how it made them nervous to walk down that hallway. Maybe a coach explains that the students will not be able to play in the next game and that could cost them a chance at the playoffs. So many times we have seen students, when asked again about impact after these stakeholders have shared, say something like, "Wow, I never realized how many people I affected." And now, when we move into repairing the harm, we are able to talk not about just taking actions to repair the relationship between the two students who fought, but also about repairing their relationship with fellow students and family members and staff. This never fails to be a powerful moment, one where we realize the power of our actions to affect a wide range of people, both positively and negatively. This activity, stakeholders sharing about impact, is absolutely designed to make a student feel powerful and empowered as well as gaining respect for how their power can hurt or heal those around them; this is powerful learning that is not usually part of the core curriculum.

Even in some schools that are committed to RJ or SEL there is a chance that this opportunity for growth and learning is being missed, at least in part because much of the work is done in a "black box," behind closed doors. If a student is removed from class by a teacher and sent to some sort of RJ room, great circles, discussion, and harm repair may be occurring. But if the teacher and others who were involved in the incident are not invited or informed of what is happening, they may still experience the same stressful event of the student returning without a resolution or clarity around how things will move forward. They may have no idea what restorative work took place, and will not feel like the issue has been adequately resolved. In cases where all stakeholders cannot be present, communication about what restorative measures occurred is crucial.

If the system doesn't include all stakeholders, there is also a great chance for re-victimization. If the broader group of folks impacted are not included in conflict resolution, they may be harmed again. This means inviting parents, other adults, and students affected, and sometimes even the broader community outside of the school to join the process. This will ensure that not only the blossom of conflict is dealt with, but also that the roots are exposed and resolved. Sometimes this occurs through mediation, sometimes through an act of apology or a mix of these things as well as more traditional or mandated consequences. Sometimes consequences are agreed on to include actions that will address an underlying issue that might be fueling harmful behavior—attending drug or alcohol treatment or support groups, working with a teacher on creating a resume to find work, counseling, and many other actions that do not look like traditional punishments but are nonetheless demanding of time and commitment and have the potential to help a person become healthier and better able to be a productive and safe part of the community with a decreased motive to re-commit harm. Wouldn't working with a teacher after school to apply for jobs be a better consequence for stealing than sitting after school in silent detention with that same teacher? Wouldn't it be such a missed opportunity to show that theft will not be tolerated, while also showing that we empathize with a young person's wants and needs and are willing to support their work to achieve these things in a more positive way?

As mentioned, the severity of the act should usually dictate the number of stakeholders gathered to address it. You would not need a 10-person circle of family and administrators for a student who has been late to class three times. Conversely, if a student brought a gun to school or publicly threatened suicide, the circle to address these higher-level issues should definitely include more than just the student, the principal, and a parent. There are no prescribed numbers here, but in general, the more severe or public the act of harm, the more community representation should be present to address it.

CHOOSING STAKEHOLDERS

So, for low-level issues such as bad language, we don't need a ton of community members there to address it. But when it comes to higher-level incidents of harm, we consistently see schools struggle with how to include a broader number of people in handling the conflict. In fact, a lot of folks will agree that more stakeholders do need to be involved in these cases, but the logistics seem far too difficult to make it happen within their current discipline systems. People will object to devoting the time and staff resources to this type of process, or they will protest that confidentiality would be compromised. The reality is that we have the ability to address all of these concerns and this work is far too important and has proven far too effective not to prioritize this effort. The benefit is hearing from a variety of community members that the choices the author of the harm has made are not acceptable *and* that they are still important and valuable to the community. This is incredibly important.

There are many other benefits as well to being inclusive of a wide variety of stakeholders when addressing conflict. The other young people you invite to sit in that circle get a chance to speak directly to those who have harmed them and to feel heard. This is a difficult thing to do, but also empowering. They also get to look at the author, and think, "I may be sitting in that seat some day, I could also make a choice that harms others and I can see that if I do, the community is not going to let it slide, it will be addressed in full." In this way circles or restorative conferences can be preventative. The message is seen by everyone in attendance— we take proper behavior seriously in our community *and* we are not going to toss you out on your first mistake. We are going to address what happened head on, and support you in the work that you need to do. This is why a lot of youth return from a restorative conference circle thinking, "That wasn't as scary as I thought, but I also wouldn't want to be the one sitting there under such scrutiny." We want to show that we are here to enforce expectations but also to show love and support along with making sure there is accountability and consequences. Restorative conferencing after a harm is really just about making things better, and having hard conversations. Teachers present also get to see a community issue being resolved in great depth and consequence, and to find community. They may hear from other teachers who are having the same issues with a student, and new connections and strategies for improvement can be conceived. When a teacher referral is dealt with by only a dean or vice principal and the student simply returns to class after some punishment, there is not a lot of room for teachers to put their heads together, to feel that they are not alone, and to find solutions.

It can be very isolating when harmed, and it is immensely comforting to feel that there are other people in the community who care, if not people who may be experiencing the same thing with the same student(s). Victims can feel alone and not valued, and seeing others show support and concern is a huge step in the right direction for creating a connected community, one that feels all are worthy of love, belonging, and repair when harmed.

If we really are committed to creating a community of compassion, getting more stakeholders to the table is really the key to the kingdom. Training young people and families and staff to engage in these hard conversations in strong but loving ways is essential, getting the messaging across that, yes, you have an impact on those around you, but no, you are not "bad." We all make mistakes, and no, you are not getting removed or banned from the community. We just have work to do before we can move forward from what has happened.

Empower the author and the victim
Give voice to the perspectives and input of those most directly connected.

Restorative processes allow the author of a harmful act to take an active role in determining the outcome. This doesn't mean that they get to solely determine the outcome or that the victim does, but rather, that both parties (as well as other stakeholders) are taking active roles in determining the outcome. This is such an important way to think about this work. It is the collaborative repair of harm, multiple impacted parties working together to find solutions and resolutions that serve everyone's best interests. You will hear us talk about "acts of apology" that are often employed after a harm has occurred. These are not just the words "I'm sorry"; these apologies are actionable and measurable (see Chapter 10). They are commitments that the author makes, things they will actually *do* to help make things right. The best ones have defined terms and timelines, and will show an investment of time and energy towards a task that will demonstrate commitment to improving future behavior or directly repairing harm to others.

We see three issues occurring in traditional justice systems:

- Victims rarely participate in the process.

- Punishment rarely facilitates healing for the victim.

- Authors can be victims, or feel like victims, in punitive justice systems.

The way that RJ counteracts these issues is to involve young people in the process as participants, and to have them feel valued in determining outcomes. Especially with authors, we need to create spaces of accountability, and not use shame and blame or illogical consequences to make them feel like victims. If the author feels like a victim of a system, they will rarely be willing or capable of offering authentic acts of apology or of generating empathy towards those they have harmed.

Empowering the author and the victim often feels like we are focusing on the author, so it is extremely important that we also focus on empowering the victim. Sometimes you go through a great restorative process—you have authentic apologies and commitments to positive actions. But those words and those agreements are not completed; there is no follow-through by the author. Even in these unfortunate circumstances where the author does not do the work that they have agreed to do (and that is something that must be addressed with the author), there may still have been some benefit for the victim to be a part of this process. It can be very beneficial for a victim to have a space to say out loud, "Hey, it hurts me when you do this. I don't like it. I want you to stop." That practice, when properly supported, where they are able to advocate for themselves, can be transformational for someone harmed. It can be a way to take their power back, to practice brave communications, and to feel heard and valued when they may not have felt that way in the past, either by the author, the school, or both. Just the act of saying the ways you were hurt out loud, and demanding that this be stopped, can be extremely powerful.

For example, in many cases of violence between young people in a romantic relationship, this is a learned skill of strength. It is so easy for adults to think (or say), "Why wouldn't they just tell him to stop?" or "Why did she put up with that?" If young people don't have a chance to practice navigating conflict and advocating for themselves, they may fail to speak up when it really matters. The restorative process allows this practice; even if the author fails to follow through, the victim has gained a louder voice, a chance to be heard, and essential practice at speaking up for themselves, establishing boundaries, and letting those around them know that these boundaries will not be compromised. This is hard, even for most adults, and restorative conversations are a rare opportunity to actively practice these skills. If students had the chance, from elementary, through middle and high school, to practice saying, "No, that's not okay," "No, I have boundaries," "No, that doesn't feel right," they are far more likely to be able to have these tough conversations and navigate difficult situations throughout life. These types of statements are made in many implicit and explicit ways during restorative conferences. This practice goes a long way towards young people leaving school as fully formed adults in the community. It is hard for adults not to be impressed when they meet students who are a product of years of restorative practices and conferencing in school. They often shock us with their level of maturity, self-reflection, and unwavering advocacy for themselves and those they care about.

We think of this principal largely around the acts of apology that follow acts of harm. When the harm is significant we remind ourselves and others to "not just talk about it, but be about it." The fact that victims and authors are able to be collaborators when deciding the actions that will repair a certain harm is extremely empowering to both. And, as we have stated, the process empowers the victim by allowing them to practice speaking clearly in the face of harm and conflict, and growing in that skillset. It creates a space for the community to say clearly to the victim, "We hear you, that was not okay, and we support you and back you up. We acknowledge the strength it takes to say these things out loud, and we are going to be by your side to make sure you don't have to say these things alone, or go through this again." And we absolutely must remember how difficult it is to speak up against someone or a system that has been victimizing you, especially for folks facing racial, gender, or economic conflicts after having a long history of victimization in these areas. We must be extremely careful to properly facilitate these circles and conferences to honor and support the courage that is needed to make a victim's voice heard.

Value empathy
Using vulnerability to move the conflict away from shame towards empathy.

Dr. Brené Brown is a well-known leader in this work of empathy, and obviously we draw a lot from her research and writing in this area. Dr. Brown says that the most accurate measure of courage is vulnerability.[7] If young people feel safe, they are going to be vulnerable. They are going to tell you how they feel, they will tell you about their fears. And every kid, especially authors of harm, has fear. They often have deep-rooted fears of not belonging or of not being accepted by the community, even before they cause harm. So how they deal with these feelings is by putting up roadblocks, pretending apathy, which can turn into real apathy. They resist, rebel, etc. They put up barriers to prevent us from

7   www.ted.com/talks/brene_brown_listening_to_shame

connecting with them. They find other kids who are disengaged; they find other adults who are disengaged. They cause harm to feel more powerful, for attention, and to get a reaction. How we get them to engage is by making the effort to connect with them. We believe deeply that we are healthier, smarter, and better by every other positive measure when we are in a community. We are able to be more ourselves when we are together. Young people are acting in search of a community. So if school doesn't feel like a place that they belong, that's a confusing message. They may want to be in school for many reasons, but also get the feeling that it is not for them. So what are they to do? They reject this community—they reject school before school can reject them. It's just easier to say, "Forget this, I'm out" when you fear that you don't belong or that you will fail in some way.

How we get over this comes back to our ability to be vulnerable. Just like any SEL, adults in schools have to be good at this themselves. We have to be good at modeling vulnerability if we hope to evoke it in our students—connecting and empathizing with each other before we attempt to do it with our students. Kids have PhDs in bullshit detection. If we are pretending that we care, if we are only pretending that we want to connect, they will sniff it out immediately. So we need to practice ourselves, amongst our staff, whether it's at staff meetings or department meetings, wherever it can occur, we have to let down our guard and connect authentically. If we are asking students to share deeply but we are not willing or able to do so ourselves, this is basically disrespectful and sends the wrong message.

We fondly remember working with a principal who would often facilitate deep and vulnerable sharing conversations and activities in staff meetings. We remember this principal crying on a few occasions due to the vulnerability and sensitivity he modeled in his sharing and responses. It sent a powerful message to the whole staff: "I expect you to go deep, and I will be standing right here next to you, doing the same, because this is a safe space and through these discussions we will be better and stronger as a staff."

If we are able to model and create spaces in our schools where students and staff feel safe to practice being vulnerable, places to experience and build empathy, they will be far more likely to make strong connections and take accountability for their actions.

Develop agency
Encourage youth to create their own internal locus of control and define what they need or want.

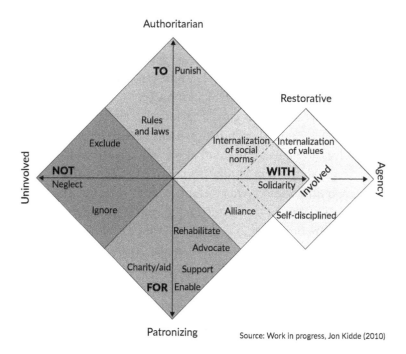

Source: Work in progress, Jon Kidde (2010)

Agency is a person's ability to shape and control their own lives, freeing themselves from the "oppression of power," to be able to accumulate power and wield it in the world to achieve your goals.

Take a look at the diagram and see the ways that discipline or addressing harm can occur in schools, and within families for that matter. In many schools we have a version of the authoritarian system seen at the top, where rules and laws are enforced by punishments that happen *to* the student. You are handed a detention if you break rule X, Y, or Z. In some cases (seen left) we have a lack of consequence, or poorly enforced values, uninvolved or ineffective leadership. This is where students are ignored or neglected, and there is a lack of a response to harm. Often this is a dangerous environment. At the bottom we have a patronizing system, and this is often (but not exclusively) seen with our youngest students. There is a lot of support, but very little responsibility or ownership is given to the students involved. Imagine a student is caught writing graffiti in the bathroom and a parent comes to the school, tells the principal that they will set up community service at their church, take the student there every Sunday, and report back on how it is going. You can see how this may not have the same impact as if the student were the driver of the restorative process. Which brings us to the quadrant on the right where the work with a young person, either after a harm has occurred or in any area of their development, happens in collaboration, where the expectation is that *they* will be the one to reflect on their actions and share the impact, as well as to participate in repairing that harm through action and apology. The adults involved are allies, helping to maintain high expectations and community values and providing support so that the student can discover the meaning of their actions and a way to make things right. This is an involved and inclusive restorative system that encourages the development of agency.

Our goal is to be doing things *with* students

The reality is that young people are going to be heading out into the world. We want them to be good human beings and citizens of their community, without adult supervision. This is why allowing them to be part of these processes of harm repair at a young age is incredibly important. We are asking them to join the adults at the table and to slowly take more and more control and accountability, as they are developmentally able. Building these skills will help them to navigate the world for the rest of their lives, having the confidence to speak up for themselves, to articulate their boundaries and goals, and to take action where it is needed to improve their relationships and outcomes.

We want to live in a world where people don't steal or commit murder or sell drugs because it is the wrong thing to do, not simply because it is against the law. We want students to refrain from causing harm, not simply because it breaks school rules or will result in a detention—we want them to behave well because it is in their best interests and they see the value of being a positive member of a community they love. That's being restorative. When we instill self-discipline in kids, where they discover an internal locus of control, it is a powerful gift.

RJ, project-based learning, and internships all share the power of experiential learning. You can learn about RJ or social and emotional growth or talk about college and careers, but until you are actually doing these things, in real time, after a harm occurs, or out at a real-world internship, or when creating your own independent project, it will not be as real and impactful. Actual practice and experience is where true transformational learning occurs; it happens when a real-world situation demands our own growth, and we are presented with an opportunity to rise to the challenge.

As we grow from not having agency to developing this important skillset, a shift occurs in the locus of control. It shifts inward, moving from relying on others for guidance to relying on ourselves. A great way to check yourself when doing restorative work with youth is to ask ourselves, "How much of the responsibility am I taking on and how much am I turning over to the young person involved? Is this my problem to fix or theirs?" By asking these questions you can be reminded to find ways where the young person can take more ownership of the work, even if it would be far easier to do it for them. This will be helping them to internalize the locus of control.

It is a cliché to tell a young person, "If you have a problem, tell an adult." While this can be great advice, what often happens is that we get young people saying, "Hey, you are an adult, please fix my problem." The teacher will then take the student(s) they are in conflict with, pull them privately into a room, and essentially say,

"Hey, Ivan, or Rene, or Genesis, stop doing what you are doing, it is hurting people," and the other student who complained is sitting isolated in the other room, unaware of what has happened. And now the student(s) who was causing harm comes out of the room, angry and upset that they got "ratted out" and the problem can often just get worse. That's precisely why victims of harm often avoid sharing with adults, even ones they trust—they have learned that it will not really help them. Even if that adult-led intervention worked, as it sometimes does, we have done nothing to help that student navigate conflict on their own. It is still the right thing to tell an adult, and speaking up like that is definitely showing courage, but we hope that in these cases the adult will not simply handle the issue themselves, but rather, employ restorative practices that encompass all the principles of RJ: realizing that conflict is a part of life, involving the stakeholders, and empowering the author and victim in resolving the issue in a real and meaningful way that will help develop their sense of agency, creating a space for empathy and vulnerability. In this way, we, as adults can stand firm on our school rules and principles while working collaboratively with students to find solutions and meaningful consequences.

Other key restorative justice ideas

While not explicitly the five pillars, the following points—about what we mean by discipline, and about how this is not so much about changing the students as about changing ourselves—are well worth noting as you proceed through this book.

What is discipline?

Discipline is really about choosing between what I want most and what I want right now.

What we want most for young people is for them to be happy and successful in life. This might include educational attainment, being engaged with their community, engaged with their school, engaged with their family. Caring about the world. Being lifelong learners. Having the skillsets they need to be successful in the world, whatever those measures of success may be for them. Whether that is securing financial stability, having a loving family, having a political voice, causing positive change in the world, creating something that they are proud of, or any number of combinations of goals. This is what we always hear from schools and teachers. This is what we often hear from teachers when asked what they want for or from kids. These are longer-term goals. But what gets in the way is what we want *right now*. Which is, "I want them to sit down," "I want them to quiet down," "I want them to raise their hand," "I want them to line up," etc.—all these things that orbit around compliance. So it is important that we consider, before we even start discussing discipline reform, what it is that we mean when we talk about discipline. It is actually a complex topic. We believe that the only real discipline is self-discipline. Let that sink in. Much like we believe that only you can hold yourself accountable, the only true discipline comes from within. Everything else is simply compliance and control. And the goal of all behavioral management is really about helping to manifest self-discipline in members of the community. Rather than thinking about disciplining children in schools, we offer that you consider instead working towards creating spaces where self-discipline can be practiced and improved through actions and consequences that promote this essential life skill.

So, as teachers, we need to remind ourselves, "What do I want most for this kid?" and consider if we are engaging with an immediate problem in a way that maximizes our long-term impact on this student. Or are we getting lost in our immediate goals, disciplining in a way that solves the immediate problem (lateness, wearing a hat, not raising a hand, etc.) that jeopardizes what we want for this person long term (graduation, a love of learning, knowledge of self, career skills, etc.)? Are we throwing away the big picture for immediate compliance?

Less changing them, more changing us

We need to stop thinking about how we are going to change children, and start thinking about how we are going to change ourselves. We need to create an environment where, through our behavior, we are changing the outcomes and experiences of young people, because it is ultimately the experiences that young people have that changes their trajectory, their path. It's not about "I need to fix this kid" or "This kid is broken," but rather how we can create an environment where the child can grow and flourish. And if we are not doing that, then that is on us, not the child. This is not to excuse harmful student behavior; just to keep focused on what we can do to create the best spaces for their success or agency after a failure. RJ is really about adult work and not about changing kids or getting them to comply. This is a huge paradigm shift for some educators, and often a hard pill to swallow, especially for folks who feel totally overwhelmed with the demands of the job. And absolutely, the demands of adults in classrooms, or adults running schools, are huge, with incredibly high stakes. And yet, we cannot shy away from the fact that our job pertaining to discipline is not to extract compliance from students, but rather to create environments where students feel valued and included, and can grow into their best selves, even after making mistakes.

3

Conflict

Conflict is often thought of as a difference between two points of view. It's a concept that is widely accepted, rarely examined, and seemingly simple to understand. But we propose that it is often misunderstood, and a great deal of energy is wasted pushing back against conflict in unhealthy and ultimately futile ways.

People often think of conflict as a heated disagreement or an argument. We are going to challenge this basic characterization. The way the word "conflict" is often used doesn't capture the complexity and variety of conflicts we experience. It often omits, for example, the pain we experience within ourselves when we fail to reach a goal, or when we give in to a habit we are trying to break. Society's discourse around conflict often omits the systemic issues of inequality and oppression. It hardly captures the intense level of pain and anger we often experience when conflicts arise with family and those we love. We have to rethink how we use and define conflict.

We are going to offer you a different definition, one that widens the concept enough to capture the vast array of conflicts we experience in our lives:

> Conflict is an exceptionally personal experience! Conflict is when my expectation does not match reality.

This new definition is deceptively simple, so we are going to restate it again clearly:

> Conflict is when my expectation does not match reality.

Think on that for a moment. What we are saying is that every time we experience painful conflict, it is because of two things—one, we had an expectation about what was "supposed" to happen, and two, that reality did not match up with that. Try it out for yourself. We might get mad at a child because we expected their room to be cleaned and it was not. Some instances seem very obvious and highly justifiable. Imagine that you lent someone money, and you agreed on a date for it to be returned. If they do not return the money, you may find yourself in conflict with that person. Seems pretty obvious. Others are more subtle and confounding. Imagine pounding your steering wheel in frustration as you encounter a huge line of traffic on your way to work. Can you see it at play there? You unknowingly held the expectation that the route would be clear and felt anger as reality presented a different circumstance that will probably make you late. It even happens internally. If someone looks in the mirror and does not like their body, it might be because they have an expectation that they *should* be thinner, more muscular, taller, not so tall, or in some way looking different than the reflection they see at that moment. These examples are not to say that all expectations are wrong, or that we should not expect our debts to be repaid; it is just a first step to illuminating the fact that *any time* you find yourself in conflict, feeling frustrated or angry, it is because there were one or more expectations that were not met. Just realizing this concept can be immensely eye-opening and helpful to how we engage with conflict.

You may hear of Buddhist teachings that talk of the elimination of expectations (or desires) as a way out of suffering and towards peace or even enlightenment. While not having expectations is a wonderful way to end personal suffering, it is truly impossible, except perhaps for the Buddha himself or any other enlightened beings that seem pretty rare in history. For the rest of us, we experience countless conscious and unconscious expectations on a daily basis. It would, however, greatly improve our quality of life and state of happiness to reduce the number and severity of the expectations we have, or at least increase our conscious awareness of them. Through thoughtful awareness we can reduce and reflect on our expectations as we recognize them in times of conflict to create a healthier relationship with ourselves, with others, and with the environment.

Two helpful ways of thinking about conflict are to divide them up into five different groups of reactions to conflict and three different types of conflict.

Five different groups of reactions to conflicts

According to the Thomas-Kilmann Conflict Mode Instrument (TKI), used by human resources (HR) professionals around the world, there are "five major styles of conflict management—collaborating, competing, avoiding, accommodating, and compromising."[1]

A metaphor that Nicholas loves to use with this is that conflict is about a pie, because we all love a good pie.

The *conflict avoider* will say there is no pie. And that's actually what we do with a lot of our conflict. "It's not a problem or a real issue," we will say! But it is, and we are actually just pretending that it is not. And this repression can be harmful to us, as we don't process our emotions. It can also lead others to not even realize that they are stepping all over us. A lack of communication can only fuel the conflict, as we grow in resentment of people who may not even be aware that they are harming or disturbing us. Years later we will wonder why we're so upset—we will lack the self-reflection to see the pie.

---

1 See https://kilmanndiagnostics.com/overview-thomas-kilmann-conflict-mode-instrument-tki

The *conflict accommodator* will say that there is a pie, but there is no problem. "You want this pie? Sure, here you go, just take it. It's your pie." We have seen this to be extremely common amongst teachers we've worked with. People who are accommodating will simply take on whatever is asked of them in order to avoid conflict, or will work hard to give parents, students, and administrators everything they are asking for. This usually comes with the best intentions, but can greatly contribute to burn-out. When there are demands placed on them by the principal, or a student needs extra help, they may simply say, "Okay, that's not a problem, I'll stay late or work on it over the weekend." This can be problematic long term for mental health, for example.

On the opposite side are *competitors*, who will say: "It's my pie, I'm going to take that pie." Classic aggressive statements would include: "That's your problem, not mine. I'm going to do what I want and you can just deal with it." This conflict style poses obvious challenges to relationships, as often aggressively demanding things can disrupt caring relationships.

The final two types of conflict are much more nuanced.

The *conflict compromiser*—"Let's cut the pie in half" or "Let's cut the pie 60/40, or even 10/90." Either way we are splitting it; even if it is an unfair split, it is offering that they get some and others get some as well. In the grand scheme of things this is often what we do when working with young people. Here is everything we would like from them, but also, here is what they may be developmentally capable of at this point, so we reach a compromise, realizing that they may be reaching some of our expectations but not all of them. Compromising is great and it is what would result in students not getting a perfect 100 percent in a course, but also not 0 percent. Most students would fall into this middle area of academic achievement.

While the *conflict collaborator* says: "Hey, let's work together to bake a bigger pie. Or let's make two pies and we can each have one!" This is a great approach, but can also take much more time and resources to achieve. When given the space, time, and resources this can be the most fruitful style, but it is also the most time- and relationship-intensive.

There is a general idea that all of these conflict styles are normal and can work, but also that some are usually much more effective and successful than others. Of course, sometimes there is a need to lead without compromise. If a student is running out into a busy street, there is no compromise in that moment—you have to act to keep them safe. Or if a student is getting into a fight in the hallway, there is no room for accommodating the fight, or walking away and avoiding it. Obviously you would engage in these instances in a pretty competitive, direct action sort of a way. But given time, after these immediate crises have subsided, how, then, are we going to handle these issues, this conflict? And this is where, if the time and resources are available, the best way to engage in conflict comes in, the way prescribed by RJ philosophy, which is, collaboration—let's work together to repair harm, restore relationships, build skills, and most importantly, grow from the experience.

In addition to these five groups of attitudes, there are three different types of conflict: interpersonal, intrapersonal, and systemic. We will take a look at the differences between these now.

Three different types of conflict
Interpersonal conflict

As we often speak and think about conflict as a disagreement or argument, we will start unpacking these ideas first. We want you to think about a conflict, any conflict, that is really present for you. It could be with a partner or maybe it is with your own children; maybe it is a constant conflict with your parents or in-laws. We know that those relationships are most often ripe with love, commitment, and conflict. These examples above are only a tiny fraction of the conflicts we may have with others. Other family conflicts may include:

- Division of housework: who takes out the trash, who washes dishes, who cleans the yard, who cleans the toilet.

- Childrearing: who helps with homework, who disciplines, who sets the expectation, who gets the kiddos ready for bed or school.

- Our own children: getting ready for school, cleaning up after themselves, being polite or respectful to their elders.

- With our parents and in-laws: who has a role in parenting, how to celebrate holidays, how to make dinner, issues around borrowing money or financial decisions.

We typically engage in these conflict discussions with the sense of being right. Perhaps we feel that our kids are in the wrong for not cleaning their room. Remember, we are not saying don't have expectations; just that often we need to check our expectations. Is it reasonable for me to expect my five-year-old to eat all their food every time? Is it reasonable for my seven-year-old to pick up their toys the first time I ask? The answer to both those questions is no, those aren't reasonable expectations. Just like it is not reasonable to expect that there will never be traffic on my way to work. Expectations are not evil, they are part of being human, and in fact, many of our expectations are reasonable and fair and foster kindness and trust between people.

Our expectations of our spouses and co-parents with whom we share the household chores and childrearing responsibilities are reasonable, most of the time. Our challenge to you isn't "don't have expectations" but instead "think about your conflicts and the underlying expectations that are driving them." Try to clearly articulate your expectations, to others or to yourself. Maybe you didn't like the way your partner was acting at a dinner party—you could easily point out things that upset you. But are you clear about how you would have liked them to act in those social situations? Have you had that conversation clearly? Have you listened to your partner's reaction to hearing those requests? Sometimes a huge amount of time and energy can be saved by understanding your own expectations and making them explicitly clear to others.

David often shares a story about a young high school couple who had a public argument in the hallway over some pictures posted on social media of the boyfriend with another girl sitting on his lap. The boyfriend thought he was not at fault because he didn't kiss or "touch" this girl who was obviously flirting with him, whereas the girlfriend thought he was a total jerk for letting the girl sit on his lap like that. Obviously, they had different expectations about how a partner should act at a party.

We love this exploration of how expectations influence our conflicts. Now take this idea into the classroom. First, what are the conflicts that we normally have in classrooms?

- Safety: keep your hands to yourself, don't throw things, play nicely at recess, don't play with the Bunsen burner.

- Respect: don't swear, listen when I am talking, respect other people.

- Engagement: sit down, raise your hand, be "on task," ask questions, track with your eyes.

We notice that many of our conflicts are grounded in compliance, an expectation that youth are going to do what we say when we say it with a sense of urgency. If that were the case we would be in boot camp. Nicholas should know because he was in boot camp many decades ago and that was the formula for success. We continue to ask ourselves and others, are these reasonable expectations of students? Often we would say no, but this does not excuse us from looking for a high standard or supporting students to reach that standard. Again, the secret to success is examining our expectations (often we don't even realize what they are) and making them clear to those we engage with. Better to have a discussion with your class about an expectation *before* it is broken. And that expectation should go both ways—what we expect of our students as well as what the students expect from us, their teachers. This information will be extremely helpful in avoiding potential conflicts.

Intrapersonal conflict

We want to re-stress to you the idea that "conflict is expectation not meeting reality." This is a very helpful way of talking about all types of conflict. In RJ conversations we often get distracted by explosive or public displays of conflict. These look like fights or arguments; sometimes it looks like property damage or other harmful crimes. We also experience, both personally and with students, intrapersonal conflict.

Intrapersonal conflict is the conflict that resides within ourselves. This is the conflict of not being good enough, smart enough, or thin enough. It is easy to say, "You are enough," but this doesn't change the fact that sometimes we still feel deficient.

The intrapersonal conflict that comes up for teachers the most..."I'm not a good enough teacher." This deep-seated self-doubt undermines our ability to engage with students. It tears at the fabric of how we think about ourselves and our work, especially when a class is chaotic or a particular student isn't responding. How we discuss conflict is extremely important, as well as what expectations we have of ourselves.

In our teaching practice we are led to believe that if we are good enough teachers, we won't have disruptive students. If we are good enough teachers, our pedagogy will be so engaging that students will never be bored or distracted. You are reading this and laughing because you know that this is silly, and yet, many teachers, somewhere inside, believe it.

There are other ways we can think about intrapersonal conflict. If I am in a meeting and I'm not being heard, I might think that there is something wrong with me; what I've said isn't the "right" thing or it's not smart enough for my principal to recognize. Remember, conflict is about the expectations we have of others and of ourselves. But, as mentioned, if we can do the hard work to recognize the self-expectations we hold, especially if they are ridiculous, we can do a much better job of staying calm and working through internal conflict.

Systemic conflict

The third type of conflict is systemic conflict—it's possible to do equity work without focusing on RJ, but you just can't have RJ without equity. While not all systemic conflict is an equity issue, we want to make sure we enter this conversation about systemic conflict with equity in the front of your mind.

We work from a comprehensive equity lens including 10 aspects of culture:

- Race

- Ethnicity

- Gender identity

- Sexual orientation

- National origin

- Language

- Age

- Socio-economic status

- Physical or mental ability

- Religion.

These factors impact how we make meaning in the world. While we will pull these ideas apart in great detail in a later chapter (see Chapter 10), we need to make the connection here to systemic conflict.

Root yourself in the definition of conflict again, "when my expectations don't match up with reality." Now let's connect this to the world. What expectations do most of us have of the world?

- People will be treated equally regardless of their gender, skin, national origin, etc.

- People will have the same access to resources (college, jobs, housing) regardless of their age, religion, physical or mental ability.

- People will be able to navigate this city or town regardless of their physical ability or language.

It is remarkable that we walk through the world with all of these expectations and rarely, if ever, are they met. Most folks are able to have hard conversations about the interpersonal. This is the most familiar, although, of course, we often struggle to honestly discuss our conflicts articulately. Some of us are even good at having reflective conversations about harmful youthful behavior or thoughts. But what we're not usually good at is finding solutions when students ask, "Why is the world racist?" or "How can I help people not to be homophobic?" or "Why does the world treat us [people in wheelchairs] like we don't exist?"

One of the most powerful ideas in RJ is that it is our job to build agency and empower others to cause change in their own lives, rather than for us to fix problems for others. When students struggle with homophobia in their community, we don't get to tell them that we will fix it—not only is that a lie, but it disempowers students. What we can ask is how they would like to get involved in creating change. What we can do is suggest local organizations and groups that we are aware of as possible allies in this work. We do, however, get to be their support, their collaborators.

The clash of interpersonal and systemic conflict

Now comes the interesting intersection between a student's youthful misbehavior and systemic injustices! Sometimes a young person will get into a fight with another student—a real knock-down drag-out fight. You get them apart and after a bit of cooling down you sit with one student and ask, "What was going on?" He says, "F*** that guy, he's a f****** racist and deserves to get his a** beat." Now we have been told we have to make a choice—do we engage with the allegations of racism or do we talk about the fighting? Fighting is bad, but so is racism... What do we do?

This is a false choice; you can deal with both the interpersonal and the systemic conflict. It is going to take time to process all this, which is unavoidable, but it will be worth it. Don't let people tell you that you have to stick to the fight and look at that aspect alone. We would argue that you *can't* just stick to the fight. If you don't talk about the racism you will have these kids back in the office in less than two weeks.

Let's keep it real. We have teacher–student conflicts just like this. The student blows up at a teacher, yelling, threatening, throwing things, and calling the teacher racist. There is no pretending that you can deal with the issues of the student's behavior and not with the accusations. The two issues are walking hand in hand. This is not to say that all accusations of racism are valid, but the perception of racism is arising from somewhere, either from the accused or sometimes with unresolved issues within the accuser. In either case, there is something important to be unpacked.

Move towards conflict

We live in a world where we run or fight every time conflict is present. This is understandable. Our brains are designed to do one of those two things, in addition to freezing up entirely. When humans feel threatened we fight or move quickly towards the conflict, freeze, or pretend the conflict doesn't exist, or take flight and run away. While these tend to serve us well in high-stakes life and death decision-making situations, they don't serve us very well in most conflict situations that we're presented with in our classrooms and schools, in relationships, or in the criminal justice system.

We need to get more comfortable being in conflict, seeing others in conflict, and moving calmly towards that conflict, staying peacefully engaged in that conflict until we find solutions. How can we become more comfortable with conflict? Restorative practices! While RJ is the over-arching philosophy, restorative practices are those strategies, approaches, and programs we put in place to get better at relationships and navigating conflict.

Some of the small practices we'll speak about later in this

book (see Chapter 4) are designed to help you adjust the way you may talk about the conflicts in your space, things like, "I hear a lot of hurtful language in our classroom" or "I noticed that before lunch and at the end of the day our classroom is really messy." These non-evaluative responses to conflicts are essential practices for us and for the students we work with. When we ask questions of students about the conflict and take ourselves out of the problem-solver role, we not only enable ourselves to enter conflict with a calmer mind, we also allow students to develop these essential skills that help them address their own conflicts. By learning to be more objective about conflict, they gain perspective and are able to think more clearly and rationally about what choices to make.

Wouldn't it be nice to have students come to us with a problem such as, "Someone is saying bad things about me behind my back" and all they would want from us is support or supervision when they talk with the other student about their issue? Imagine if they had those skills. Now imagine them years later in college—are they making healthy choices? Do they understand the impact of their actions on themselves, others, and the community at large? Wouldn't they have a better chance at these outcomes if they learned to be calm, aware, and empowered in the face of conflict? And it is precisely these real-world experiences that make learning stick—real emotions, real problems. We have great opportunities in each and every conflict that a student faces for us to help create deep and lasting neural pathways that will help guide them throughout their adult lives.

Forget about *right vs. wrong* and *good vs. bad*

It is important to note that these terms are often unhelpful in addressing most conflicts. In fact, entering with that mindset (there's that word again) will only create more conflict. Try, instead, to enter the situation with both the health of the relationship and the conflict in mind. For example: "I want to support this student's learning *and* address the issue with their headphones."

We recommend not entering that conversation with the idea that this person with the headphones is doing something wrong and that we are going to make them do the right thing. Even if there is an established school rule around headphone use, and you could simply enforce that rule with a traditional consequence, imagine what would happen if you approached it from a more restorative angle: "Mike is using his headphones and it's really hurting his progress on the lesson today. I know that he wants to become a doctor someday; maybe I'll talk to him about how important this Biology class is to that future" or "Mike is working well with his headphones on, but it is distracting other students. How can we address the impact of headphones as a class?" This mindset shift is going to be helpful in reducing some of the intensity around our most common issues and will ideally help students to better understand the rationale behind the rules we establish.

For the record, there are some things that are right and wrong. We don't think it's ever a good thing to intentionally hurt others. And there are facts, of course. Gravity works, don't argue about that. Speed is measurable, and not wearing your seatbelt can kill you. The problem isn't with these types of discussions. The problem is when it comes to tastes, preferences, interpretation, and feelings. When you focus on who's right and who's wrong you will likely lose track of the relationship. It not only doesn't matter who's right, but it can, in fact, be harmful to the relationship if it is about being right or wrong. Approaching Mike about him being wrong for wearing his headphones, or Mike approaching you as wrong for enforcing this rule that he finds silly, usually won't lead anywhere restorative. We urge you to think instead about impact, about relationships and communicating expectations.

We are asking you to try and forget about good and bad. Try that on. Some folks say that all kids are good, but doesn't "good" by definition mean there must also be kids who are "bad?" If I am able to shift away from good and bad towards a belief that all kids are humans who need care and education, I am better equipped, mentally and emotionally, for the most challenging students. Kids and adults are doing their best. And as hard as it is to keep in mind sometimes, we often think of the quote, "Those who are the hardest to love usually need it the most."

In your classrooms and schools, focus on the common mission and forget about right and wrong and good and bad. Think instead about harm done. Think about conflict as an opportunity to build connection.

PUTTING MY FOOT IN MY MOUTH

A referral came in to our office from a teacher who worked in the computer lab about a student who had reportedly broken some of the computer keyboards during a free period when he should not have been in the lab. The teacher wanted to get to the bottom of it. In my interview with the student, he admitted to being in the computer lab when he should have been in the cafeteria, but he claimed that there were three or four other students there as well, and he vehemently denied breaking the keyboards. He also stated that the teacher had yelled at him for it in front of the other students and that had really upset him. I spoke with the teacher privately as well, and they both agreed to meet and discuss in mediation.

The mediation went well. We did not solve the keyboard mystery, unfortunately, but the student apologized for being in an area that he should not have been, and offered to help clean up the floor after school. The teacher explained how important the computers are to many students and how disrespected he felt to see them broken. He admitted that he could have handled himself more calmly at that moment when he addressed the student in front of the class. We even had time to discuss some of the reasons behind the student's currently failing grade in Computer Science and what he would need to do to bring it up to passing. Hands were shaken. Before leaving, the teacher asked me, "Do you want to speak to the other teacher who also works in the computer lab? I can go cover for him and send him up?" Although I had not planned on this, wanting to make sure everyone affected was involved in the restorative process, I said, "Sure, thank you, send him up." I debriefed with the student as we waited for the other teacher to join us. I was new at the school and what I didn't know was that this other teacher was not a fan of mediations like this, and was openly skeptical about the new restorative approach towards school discipline.

I could sense the tension the moment the teacher walked in and sat down at the table. Not long after I started to go over some basic protocols of our discussion, things went south. The teacher made his stance clear by saying something like, "No disrespect, but I think we are wasting our time here. Several kids say they saw him playing with the computers, so I'm not trying to hear his excuses. In fact, he barely shows up to class and that's why he is failing. That's what we should really talk about." I attempted to regain focus. "Those are valid concerns and we can get to them one by one, but I want to make sure that you both have a chance to speak and be heard before we..." The student jumped in, "I didn't break the keyboards! I saw Sandy and Mike playing with them too, why don't you..." "You're lying" the teacher fired back, "I know you are lying and it's ridiculous that I'm missing class for this." I could see that this was not working and I said so to them both. "I don't want to use this time to argue, and I hear that your teacher is concerned about missing his class, so let's pause on this process for now. I can meet with you both individually and see how we can move forward from this in a more productive way." "So I can leave?" the teacher asked in irritation. "Yes," I said.

Frankly, I was shocked by how this teacher had acted. I tried to hide this, but I'm sure the student could see it. I simply apologized to him that it didn't go as well as I expected and that we need to all be better than this in the mediation setting, but that it is normal for emotions to run hot at times. After we were done I walked back to the RJ office feeling angry at this teacher for not showing more restraint and respect as an adult and an educator. I sat down at my computer to take down some notes from the event and to clear my head.

Without getting into the details, a few days later a staff member happened to see my notes from this day and shared what I had written with the teacher from the mediation. I thought that my notes would remain private, and I was upset when I wrote them, so when I described the mediation I used some language that I really should not have. At some point I said the teacher was acting like a "childish prick." I'm not proud of what I wrote, but that's what he and some other staff ended up hearing about.

I was horrified when this was reported to me by Anea, a History teacher, who also let me know that the teacher had threatened to make an official complaint against me to the school district. I was mortified, embarrassed, ashamed, and even though I still condemned the teacher's behavior, I should have been more careful in my notes. I had not meant to make this mistake, and I genuinely felt sorry for what harm I had caused. Luckily, Anea was also trained in RJ and mediation, and had gotten the teacher to agree to let her mediate this conflict between the two of us. She told me the meeting would happen the next day. I was appreciative that the school really stood behind this RJ work, even supporting its use with staff. There are a lot of schools that ask students to engage in this process but that stick to traditional ways of dealing with conflict amongst staff members.

This school was truly acting restoratively, and I appreciated that, but I felt sick about my upcoming mediation and was convinced that many staff at the school were talking about what had happened behind my back as I walked down the hall. Not the way I wanted to help spread a positive message of RJ across the campus. It was all I could think about until we sat down the next day. The meeting was pretty straightforward. I quickly made a genuine apology for what had happened and assured the teacher that he had every right to be upset at me. It was true that I disapproved of his behavior, and I let him know that I wished he had been more respectful in the mediation, but also that I truly had acted unprofessionally in my notes and I felt horrible. Even if they were just between three people, it was wrong to write that language on a school document. He told me that he had every right to file an official complaint and wanted me to know that, which I acknowledged.

Anea did a good job of keeping us on track, and unpacking the situation. Like most mediations, I benefited from learning more about his perspective. For instance, when I was asked if I wanted "the other teacher" sent up, it seemed like an easy "yes." But all this teacher had experienced was a colleague saying, "You need to go upstairs for a mediation about what happened with the keyboards." The teacher felt disrespected by this, by the assumption that he should just drop whatever he was doing and go talk about this student, a student he really didn't feel deserved this precious time at the end of the semester after barely attending his class. I explained that I had no idea the mediation was presented that way to him, that it is always voluntary, and that I could see how that put him in a foul mindset towards the process. I really should have made sure to consult with him before I brought him into that space. That was my fault. He accepted my apology, agreed not to file a grievance, asked not to be a part of any further mediations and we left the room. I learned from Anea that he is actually a wonderful teacher who uses a lot of restorative practices and has stellar relationships with most students in his classes, but that he was skeptical of a lot of changes that were happening this year.

Despite this being my third year using restorative practices in schools, I had never been on this side of the mediation table before, in the "hot seat," and it was eye-opening. I got to see and feel what so many students experience when we ask them to engage in this work. I was anxious about the mediation. I felt ashamed and embarrassed of my actions. I was scared that I might be formally punished. I wondered who was talking about me and my mistake as I walked the hallways of the school. As sorry as I was for the whole event, it gave me a lot of empathy and compassion for the students I work with. To think that students face all of this and the repercussions of a call home to family. At least I didn't have to worry that the school was going to call my mom! I had gained a new respect for the courage and maturity youth must show in facing those they have harmed or those who have harmed them. It helped me to reflect on and refine my mediation skills.

I'd love to say that Philip and I became fast friends after this.

Although that didn't happen, our mediation gave me a greater understanding of how he was thinking and feeling as a teacher in the school, and made me feel like I didn't have to hang my head and avoid his gaze as we passed in the hallway. We ended up working together in the same space later that year and we actually had some really great discussions and debates about student discipline. It turned out that, philosophically, we really were not that different. I truly believe that without the mediation we had prior, without the apology and the listening that occurred, we would not have felt comfortable to have those conversations and to work so well together to the benefit of the students we both served. It is so easy to forget how it feels for others sitting at a mediation table or in a circle. This difficult experience resulted in not only a change in my behavior, but also allowed for my growth as a person and a community member; put simply, RJ at its best.

Story debrief

As illustrated in this story, there is a huge difference between staff learning about and even facilitating RJ, and getting to actually experience it for themselves. As awkward and difficult as it may have been to face the harm caused, by working through it in a restorative system, relationships were able to be held intact for the future, and there was personal growth in the process. It is important for staff to utilize the same practices (circles, mediation, etc.) that they are asking students to engage in. We are all equal members of the community.

4

Restorative Language

NON-EVALUATIVE AND CONFLICT STYLES

You have heard us say that we can never fully eliminate human conflict. Instead, we need to teach and learn how to engage in conflict in a healthy way, and we can even strengthen our relationships as a result of working together through conflict. This is one of the most beautiful parts of RJ philosophy: conflict can help us grow closer as individuals. Nonetheless, a lot of unnecessary conflict remains, which can be easily reduced and prevented in your life and your school.

One of the greatest tools to accomplish a reduction in conflict, and a way to communicate in the face of existing conflict, is *non-evaluative language*.

As a dean in NYC, David saw a lot of discipline referrals that resulted from situations that could have easily been de-escalated if those people involved had used more non-evaluative language. This technique is a simple and powerful tool of communication that accomplishes two things at the same time:

- It prevents us jumping to (the wrong) conclusions.

- It allows for growth in self-reflection.

As simple as it sounds to make a non-evaluative statement, it is easier said than done, and is a skill that takes practice to master.

Non-evaluative language

What exactly is non-evaluative language?

Non-evaluative language is about making an observation, and then taking a pause. This observation will be rooted in an objective, observable fact, a clear statement of reality, devoid of added opinions and judgments. We could give a thousand examples but will try to highlight a few here to make the point.

An obvious difference would be:

That student doesn't care about school (*evaluative*).

Versus

That student has been absent 10 days this month and only has a passing grade in one class (*non-evaluative*).

Notice how the first statement might be making assumptions that are inaccurate about the student's attitude towards school, whereas the second statement is rooted in measurable data. The first statement may be true to some degree, and this apathy would be a great topic to explore with the student, but it could also be totally false. The student may love school but be suffering a hardship outside the classroom that is preventing their attendance and grades from being excellent. The point is that our language is important, and we don't often have all the information to make snap judgments accurately.

Avoiding the wrong statement can make a huge difference in our relationships and in classroom management. Some clear examples of non-evaluative language would be:

I notice that you no longer sit with Alexa at lunch.

I notice that you are putting your hands on someone right now.

You didn't turn in the last assignment.

Make a statement like this, and then—*and this is so important*—just stop right there.

Make a real and intentional pause without speaking. Give the person time to reflect on your statement in an authentic way.

This is where it is extremely important that your statement is non-evaluative, and not colored with your own opinion and judgments. If you add those things, the student will all too easily be consumed with sorting through the reaction to your judgments.

Take the non-evaluative statement, "I notice you didn't sign up for basketball this year." This allows a student to share why it is that basketball will not be in their life this year. An evaluative statement would be more like, "It's so disappointing that you didn't sign up for basketball this year, the team really needs you." Now you have possibly added shame and clouded the chance for real conversation. Now the student is left thinking about how their choice has disappointed you and others. You made them feel bad before the conversation has even started. Perhaps the student's family could not afford the fees for the basketball team this year. Now you have been truly insensitive and may even evoke an explosion of anger or tears because of your assumption that it was a choice and not a hardship.

You can see how non-evaluative statements—simply stating facts that you observe—can create a space for the student to share what might be going on for them, a safe space where important information can come to light. In many examples, saying these things in the wrong way may result in a verbal altercation, but said in a restorative way, stemming from observation and connection rather than assumption and judgment, might result in a meaningful conversation and maybe even a solution to the issue at hand.

David often shares this example. A student who is frequently late walks into class, and the teacher sarcastically says in front of the class, "Miss Lee, nice of you to finally join us." Maybe some students even laugh. This rises from obvious and understandable frustration from the teacher, but can so easily result in a minor or major conflict. Often the student, if they were to curse at the teacher or flip a desk, will be punished without the teacher's comment ever being examined. This is not a healthy community built on strong relationships.

Obviously, the better route would be to speak with the student privately, but even in that setting you have the choice between a judgmental or non-evaluative statement. If you start this private conversation with, "You really need to care more about your schoolwork, you're going to fail this class," you have already added assumptions, judgment, and shaming all in one sentence! This would be the perfect time to try out non-evaluative language. Say something like, "I notice that you have been late on six occasions this month," and then wait to hear how the student responds to that simple statement.

Non-evaluative language is one of the most powerful things a student can experience. Hearing such an unclouded statement, and having that silent pause to reflect, is something many young people don't often experience. Without having their guard up, as they would with a shaming or judgmental statement, they are left with a space in which to process the information, and will usually offer an honest explanation about what is going on in their world. This is a place to show that you are a caring and concerned ally, that you have high standards and want them to attend, but that you want to hear them out and see how you can assist their success—far different from the usual lectures and threats. All too often these one-on-one conversations will reveal a serious hardship in a young person's life. They are having transportation issues, or must care for a younger sibling, or may not even have stable housing. Imagine, in these circumstances, how insulting it would be for a teacher to mock their tardiness in front of the class.

When David has felt the urge in the moment to address a student walking in late, he has found that a better way to make the same point would be something like, "Awesome, Danielle you made it! I'm so happy you didn't miss this important lesson. Jump on in with group B and I will come by to explain what you missed and give you the materials you need to catch up." This exemplifies the notion that "The class is better when we are all here. I see you, and you are valuable." And it still makes room to speak with the student about their lateness, impact, and finding solutions to the issue, all without shame or sarcasm—something David will freely admit he has been guilty of in the classroom. This is about restorative *practice*, not *perfection*, and simply acknowledging when you have not acted the way you wish you might have. All of this is about modeling, even modeling how to apologize and try again when you are not at your best.

Often when you do make a non-evaluative statement and create a space for reflection, students will surprise you with how well they share what is going on for them, volunteer helpful information, and communicate deeply. But when they don't, when they just sit there saying nothing, you can always ask a question. A restorative question works in the same way as non-evaluative language. "Is everything okay?" shows care and concern without judgment, whereas a question like, "Why aren't you making good choices this year?" carries obvious potential to harm the relationship and shuts down the conversation.

Linking non-evaluative language with classroom expectations

If we are to look at the example of a physical altercation (separating a student and saying, "I notice you are putting your hands on someone in the class"), we can then turn the question towards our expectations, which should be clear and known to all—"What are our expectations around this?" This allows the student to reflect without being directly attacked, and to evaluate their own actions. This is a core component of SEL. "We are supposed to act safely in class" would be a great bit of self-reflection in this instance. It does not yet get to the core of the conflict, but starts the student down the path of examining their actions in the moment and the impact they are having. David has done work with students in a "restorative detention" setting (see 'The Revolution that Restorative Detention Can Be' in Chapter 10 for more on this topic), using time after school with students practicing how to have a great group discussion. With five clear expectations written on a large poster board, when a student interrupts another student, rather than saying, "Don't interrupt!" or "Stop it, Mark! You're ruining the conversation," he is able to ask, "Mark, which expectation was broken right there when you jumped in?" Mark can then focus the question on the board to say, "Rule number 3, one mic. Okay, I'll wait my turn, I just have something I really want to say." And David can say, "Great, I can't wait to hear it after Sarah is finished." The relationship stays positive and new skills of kindness and self-reflection are being practiced. This is something that we do with our own children at home: "I notice that the toys are not in the basket" or "Your plate is still on the table." Often this can lead to a child taking their plate and putting it into the sink as they are expected to after the meal, without conflict or argument.

The process is built on a non-judgmental observation, and then a reflection on established expectations. This allows the true work of connecting our actions with the larger community and our own goals. Note that the expectations of the community must be clear and agreed on in advance of this conversation. The rule of "one mic" (only one person speaking at a time), for instance, must have been discussed, explained, and agreed on previously, in order for the group to consider it a valuable rule.

Young people (and adults!) are so used to people immediately telling them that their actions were good or bad, and being given praise for something done right or a lecture on what they did wrong, that the combination of a non-evaluative observation and a pause for reflection can be truly powerful, challenging, and a great way to teach the skills and language needed in a restorative system.

This brings us nicely to the topic of restorative language and questions.

Restorative language

Restorative language uses the type of statements and questions that provoke self-reflection, creating a space for accountability, empowerment, and authentic relationships. Much like non-evaluative language, restorative language should be free from shame and blame (see Chapter 5), and focused on encouraging connection, empathy, and personal accountability. This is the type of language that would be used in a restorative conference or mediation when seeking a better understanding of an incident, even if we think we already know what occurred.

These are the questions that we are constantly trying to encourage teachers and school staff to use when exploring an incident:

What happened?

What was your thinking? Or, What was motivating you?

What was the impact?

What do we need to do now to make things better?

We can see from these restorative questions, and the earlier examples of non-evaluative statements we looked at, that restorative conferencing has three stages:

1. *Objectively establish the details of the situation.* We achieve this by using *non-evaluative language* and allowing students the space to consider the actuality of the situation, rather than hiding behind a defensive wall.

2. *Push deeper into the thoughts and feelings that were happening at the time,* for the author of the harm and the people who were impacted. We achieve this through *restorative language and questions.*

3. *Consider how we can repair the situation and move forward,* ensuring it will not happen again. We achieve this through a focus on the *impact* of people's actions, encouraging self-reflection on how actions can link to impact. This can be achieved via both non-evaluative and restorative language.

This is the bread and butter of restorative conferencing.

Restorative language in practice

Let's look at a quick mediation example. Two students who are having a conflict are asked to kindly step into the hall for a quick conversation. The first restorative questions that could be asked is, "What is happening? What is going on? Why are we out in the hallway right now? Tell me more about what is going on between you two." We often presume that we know what is going on, or we assume we know the whole story, or we simply focus on the rules that are being broken, but starting from this open-ended and non-judgmental question, "Tell me more about what is going on between you two" will allow clearer conversation and resolution.

Of course, we make presumptions about what is going on between students because we often, especially those of us who have been doing this work for years, do know what is going on in many instances. Yes, you may know exactly what is going on, your presumptions may be totally correct, but this is not about you as a teacher; it is about the students, and giving them the skills to reflect and articulate what is happening for themselves.

Even if you have video footage of an incident, and you don't need any further details from the students to establish the facts, remember that this is not about *you* doing the work, but about *them* doing it.

So, we encourage folks to start with point 1 above: "What happened?" Allow them the chance to practice honesty, accountability, articulation, and the slew of other traits that it takes to recount an emotionally charged experience truthfully. Start there. Then you can get to point 2, "What was the thinking?"

Look closely at this last question: "What was your thinking at the time of this incident?" It is not, "What were you thinking!?"— that classic judgmental question, which really means, "Why were you doing what you were doing? That was bad!" In response to this question, students may give a defensive myriad of reasoning and a ton of excuses, many of them not making much sense. But we can instead use restorative language to create a calm space for true curiosity and introspection:

What thoughts were you having at the time of the incident?

What were you trying to get out of this behavior?

What were you trying to accomplish by doing this?

What were you hoping would happen?

If we do this, we can create a space for young people to realize and express their true motivations. Maybe, "I wanted him to stop teasing me" or "I wanted the teacher to leave me alone." This is the first step to them unpacking what happened. "Okay, so that is why you cursed at the teacher and left the room." "Okay, I can see that getting out of there was what you wanted, you wanted to be left alone. Ultimately, it ended up giving you more teacher attention, and we can discuss that, but at least now I understand what you were thinking and how you were feeling at that moment."

Now, if we simply ask the usual question, "Why did you curse at the teacher and walk out?" you are likely to get a response, "Because the teacher was being a bitch" or "Because he's racist and no one in this school understands me." You are not likely to get closer to an honest and calm discussion of thoughts and feelings. These will not be helpful responses to moving forward. Can you see the slight difference between, "Why did you do that?" and "What was your thinking when you did that?" The much more productive type of question is the latter, or perhaps, "What were you hoping to get out of this?" rather than "Why did you do this?" Kids grow up getting asked this question all the time. Why did you do this? Why? Why? Why!? And in a vast amount of cases, they actually have no idea why they did what they did—they lack the skills or the practice in making these types of reflections.

> By asking better restorative questions, we can show that *we are actually interested in the student's answer*, not just in lecturing them, and we can give them the time and space to start exploring and understanding their own actions, something that is likely to help prevent future conflicts for years to come.

Let's return to the previous example of non-evaluative communication: "I notice you have not turned in your assignments this week." A follow-up restorative question might then be to ask, "What type of support do you need to start getting your assignments in on time?" This is in stark contrast to a threat like, "If you don't get your assignments in on time, you will fail the class." You can see how the second type of comment could invoke stress and conflict or argument, while the restorative question, "What do you need?" accomplishes so much. It demonstrates that you care, and that you are willing to support the student as an ally. It also puts the student in the driver's seat, asking them to problem-solve and advocate for themselves. It can lead to breakthroughs on a variety of fronts, and will not usually result in a conflict the way the threat of failure often will.

A more restorative and reflective way to approach the possible failing grade would be to ask, "How are missing these assignments affecting you in this class?" The student may then be able to reflect on how their grade is suffering and may also realize that it is causing them to be confused and bored during lessons, which might be why they are being disruptive or avoiding coming to class altogether. Often, we, as adults, are obsessed with pointing out the obvious, when we could be leading students to discover their blind spots, the things that we can plainly see but they have yet to realize about their behavior. Remember: this is not about *you* doing the work; it's about *them* doing it.

Tell me what is happening.

What are the expectations around this?

How is that impacting you?

What help do you need?

These are all great follow-up restorative questions after a non-evaluative observation and an intentional pause. Allow students to process events, reflect on expectations, develop an understanding of impact, and grow in self-advocacy as they articulate what they might need. This is restorative language, and when a whole school community can communicate in this way, massive change in personal relationships is possible.

The *impact* of what we say

One of the questions we mentioned above is, "What was the impact?" This is incredibly important and is really at the core of non-evaluative language, restorative language, and RJ. It is also a skill that is often underdeveloped.

Being able to recognize the impact—both positive and negative—that we have on our community is a huge life skill to unlocking our empowered selves, and non-evaluative language and RJ can pave the way to a better understanding of the impact of our actions.

We can recount endless instances where a restorative circle was held after some type of argument or fight between two students. When asked, "Who was affected?" the answer is usually that they only impacted themselves and maybe the person with whom they had fought. Often, members of the circle will have a chance to share how they were impacted, and the students, when asked the same question at the end, will now be able to articulate:

> I can now see I impacted more than just me and the person I fought. I can see that the principal had to leave a meeting, that my mom had to leave work to come pick me up, that I scared some people in the cafeteria, that maintenance had to clean up the broken glass, etc.

This highlights the difference between RJ and traditional criminal justice systems. In punitive systems we try to encourage a behavior by putting downward or negative pressure on unwanted behaviors. If you don't want people to steal, criminalize it, and if it isn't working, increase the punishment—put them in prison for longer, be harsher. The problem is that the cost of many of these punishments is worse for us as a society. It costs a great deal of money to imprison someone, it costs dignity, it's inhumane, and it costs us lots of people—their lives, their freedom, their ability to contribute. On top of that, this type of escalating punishment is rarely effective in preventing future conflicts. By contrast, what really helps to change negative behaviors is an understanding of the impact of those actions and behaviors.

In addition, when students are not exhibiting pro-social behaviors, or meeting our expectations, we so often discipline them with disengagement—detention, suspension, removal from class. We are often multiplying an already existing condition of disengagement or of being behind on classwork with obvious negative repercussions. Even at a young age they fall behind, and the gap is insurmountable.

Understanding that people in their community are being hurt by their behavior

In the vast majority of cases, young people do not understand the impact of their behavior on themselves, the people around them, and those who care about them. Kids who bully other students online don't really have a true understanding of how this affects those they are bullying. If they did, they would be less likely to do it. David has seen this in real life. A student who is bullied opens up in a restorative classroom circle with others about hardships they are going through. Maybe it is about being teased for being overweight or an issue going on at home. Those in the circle immediately see the student in a more humane way and the bullying stops or is reduced.

Non-evaluative language and restorative questions, when used effectively with students, are a key foundation for helping them understand the impact of their behavior.

Rather than imbuing our statements with criticism or value judgments, the unbiased space created by a non-evaluative state-ment or a restorative question gives students the best possible chance of actually stopping to think—and this paves the way for them to arrive at an understanding of the impact of their actions. The language we use is at the root of everything we do in RJ.

David has often shared a photo essay from *It's Complicated: The American Teenager* by Robin Bowman.[1] The picture is of a transgender teen. Several students are often quick to make fun of or comment negatively about the portrait when it is examined in a discussion circle. But on reading the accompanying essay by this brave and outspoken young person, about being called names and being badly beaten up, this often resonates with the students. They share when they were called names or even when they themselves were beaten up. They begin to empathize with the young person and see how they have been impacted and hurt, and they are less likely to be as mean about the person as they were before.

Paving the way for students to understand the impact of their words and actions is incredibly important; using non-evaluative and restorative language in discussion circles can work wonders in achieving this. Through these circles, we can help students to see that their use of language matters. If you invite them to see things less judgmentally and pare it back to the facts alone, this allows the students a chance to have pause for thought, which opens up a space for restorative questions. This, in turn, leads to empathizing and positive takeaways going forward.

A freshman student from another class came to David to complain that he often smelled weed in his class, and he knew students were coming in high. Rather than simply taking the traditional approach of detective work to identify the culprits and punish them, David convened an impact circle. He asked the restorative question: "How do you feel when you smell weed in this class?" This was a safe space to discuss the behavior, without naming names, and how it had impacted them.

Almost no students denied that it was occurring. Some didn't have much to say; they didn't care. Some students, mostly to get a laugh or look "cool," said things like, "I love it! Weed is awesome" (and this is part of a sharing circle: you cannot always control the

---

1   Bowman, R. (2007) *It's Complicated: The American Teenager.* Brooklyn, NY: Umbrage Editions.

comments and must allow everyone to have their turn with the talking piece).

But many of the students honestly shared that they did not like to smell it in their class. They felt it was disrespectful to the teacher, who didn't deserve this, or that it was distracting. One student said, "You know, when I smell weed in the class, it reminds me of my dad." The class immediately fell silent and everyone was on the edge of their seat. He continued, "My dad has struggled with drug addiction his whole life. It's been really hard for me and my family. School is usually a place where I don't have to think about it, but when I smell weed, it just makes me sad, and I have to think about that stuff." This was a huge breakthrough in vulnerability and impact sharing for the class. David believes it was part of the reason why the problem improved. And the bravery of this student, built on the healthy restorative practices of the class, improved all their future conversations.

The restorative question, "How do you feel when you smell weed in this class?" was very effective in paving the way to the students understanding the impact of their actions.

The final question about impact after a harm has occurred, asked to yourself, to others, and the community, is, "What do we need to do now to make things better?" This might happen in depth during a conference or as a quick conversation in the hall. Answers may include, "I cannot use that language in class" or "If I'm done with my work I can sit more quietly."

Questions to ask when considering if your language or question is restorative or self-serving

- Am I inspiring self-evaluation or dependence on the evaluation of others?

- Am I being respectful or patronizing?

- Am I helping them discover how to act or am I trying to manipulate their behavior?

- Am I seeing the child's point of view or my own?

- Would I make this comment to a friend or neighbor?

These are great lens questions for restorative language when thinking about the words you are using.

Again, agency from the students is what we are striving for. *Young people have to do the work*, and we need to create spaces for them to do this work. We, as educators or adults, are such quick thinkers that we often—with the intention of helping—jump right in to tell them what to do, or to say, or lead them to an answer that we want. But we need to build self-restraint here and learn to create space and pauses for students to come to conclusions on their own and to be able to do this in the future.

The old saying, "Give a man a fish..." applies here. *Tell* a student whom they impacted, and they may get it that one time; allow them to *discover* whom they impacted, and they may gain that skill for life. Non-evaluative language and restorative questions pave the way to the students achieving this discovery. There is no *telling* in non-evaluative language or restorative questions, because they are deliberately devoid of judgment and opinion.

Other ways to recognize impact: linking non-evaluative language and restorative questions with affective statements

Affective statements can help us see how others have been impacted by a person's behavior. This is most effective in an "I" statement. They serve to separate the author from their actions, and express empathy through naming emotions. "I felt sad when I heard you say that to John," or perhaps even better, "When I heard what you said to John, I felt sad because I value respect. Would you be willing to tell me about that?" In fact, we often make "I" statements like, "I was shocked to see you act that way," which is really a YOU statement in disguise. You are really just saying, "You shouldn't act that way." Do you notice the slight difference? "I felt sad when that was said" really puts the focus on our own feelings and separates the statement from the person saying it. The word YOU is not even used at all, whereas, "I was shocked when you said that" is really a shaming statement that focuses more on the other person's behavior than our own feelings. We strive for this type of statement in mediations: "When I heard what was said, I got upset," "When I saw what had happened, I was scared," "When people are not on task, I get distracted, I get frustrated." It is really about the work to remove the YOU and to focus on the action and provide space for objective discussion and reflection. Making it about our own experience through an "I" statement makes it easier to focus on the behavior and not the person who caused the reaction. Joe Brummer has done great work to advance and humanize affective statements.[2]

How expectations can help to reduce conflict

When you first begin, you may find that trying to lead students to discover the impact of their actions on other individuals is not so effective. This is okay. We can first work on connecting back to our classroom expectations, with a statement such as, "Hey, this is how this thing you did connects to what we expect in class here"—something like, "The joke yelled out did not meet our class expectation of respect." Later, you can go back to, "This is how it affects people" and so on, but right in the moment, when a conflict is happening, we want to clearly work on connecting to the expectations. The important pre-work, along with building strong relationships, is to establish clear expectations.

---

2   See www.joebrummer.com

To state it again: *clarifying expectations is the number one way to reduce conflict.*

Mission

The reason why we have expectations is so that we can achieve our mission and goals in a productive way. Our mission should be known and made clear to teachers and students every day: educational excellence for everyone. That is the ultimate mission, although, of course, there is a lot left for interpretation in this statement.

What best serves this mission is a set of behaviors that are built on common expectations. This can be decided on and created by the community. A set of expectations that Nicholas likes is:

Be safe.

Be respectful.

Be engaged.

Be yourself.

These are four that can really provide a foundation for kids to be successful in school. It's important to reach an understanding with students that the expectations are not there to restrict them, or to be mean, but because we care about their success. That's it. What Positive Behavioral Interventions and Supports (PBIS) programs and behavioral modification programs miss so much of is the mission: rooting the expectations and rules in achieving educational excellence for everyone.

Obviously the wording of this mission may vary in some ways depending on the setting, but it is generally the ultimate goal of schools. If we have expectations that don't actually line up with that mission of educational excellence for everyone, then we need to reflect on these expectations. Are they really productive, necessary, and worth the conflict they create? Examples include wearing hats, chewing gum, eating food in class, and walking on a certain side of the hallway. This is not to say that these rules are wrong, but are you suspending kids for these infractions? How is this impacting the mission? How is conflict being generated by enforcement of these rules? It is worth reflecting on these.

A better formula would be to examine these behaviors in terms of the expectations. Is food preventing the student from being engaged? Is hallway walking behavior impacting safety? If not, you may be fighting a pointless battle. If so, you might need to clarify *why* you are choosing to address this behavior—for the *benefit* of the student, not simply as an arbitrary rule to demonstrate your authority over that student. Always try to connect back to supporting student success, and honestly evaluate your rules and enforcement through this lens: of having conversations and seeking student reflection to better fulfill your school's mission, rather than blindly enforcing rules without authentic conversation.

The student who does not have food stability at home may be eating in class for a variety of reasons. This does not mean that you have to allow it, but being hungry does not lead to academic success, so it may be worth examining (asking) the context of the situation and looking for solutions collaboratively.

Expectations are not just about our expectations of our students

To circle back to our conversations around expectations, when we are talking to a young person about their behavior, making a non-evaluative statement and asking them to connect to expectations, we are not just asking them to reflect on what our expectations are of them. We have ideally done a ton of work already, to discuss and agree on expectations that we all have of each other. True expectations are not top-down but are actually a two-way street. We must also discuss, acknowledge, unpack, and think about how young people have expectations of us. We can discuss what respect looks like for the students in class, but we should also clarify what respect would look like from the teacher. Fair is fair. And knowing our students' expectations of us can go a long way to preventing conflict.

After all, it is completely normal that young people arrive on the first day with expectations of their teachers:

What are their expectations?

Have they been made clear?

Can we agree on these expectations?

How is it addressed when a teacher does not meet these expectations?

Students are often unclear about their own expectations of staff because they have never been asked to reflect on this before. Rarely is there space for this type of question. Having to articulate their expectations can be a game changer for them and for the teachers hearing what students are expecting of them. An example that comes to mind is that a student may have an expectation of privacy, and when a teacher posts grades on a chart board, that expectation is not met. How does this situation usually play out? What skills have teachers and students developed to have a productive and calm conversation around this type of conflict?

It is extremely important to also do this work if you truly want to limit, and collaboratively work through, conflict. One of the core tenets of RJ is to create agency. If, for example, a teacher yells at a student in class:

Have we helped students to manage their emotions to respectfully speak up and say, "I don't like the way you are speaking to me"?

Have we created a culture where this type of communication can occur between students and staff?

Have we created a culture where the staff member is doing the same work on self-reflection and connecting to the expectations that we ask of our students?

This is part of the RJ mindset shift that is often hard for schools and staff: creating a safe space for accountability, building skills in restorative language, and the ability to work through conflict in a healthy and sustainable manner.

How good is your school at having tough conversations like this?

How have you prepared your young students to have these types of tough conversations?

This is where restorative practices can be a key to building those skills over time, in circles, conferences, and classroom activities. It takes work, practice, and reflection. But even more than high test scores or perfect grades, we have been most blown away when we meet a young person with this type of social and emotional skillset, the ability to reflect on their own thoughts, feelings, and behaviors, and to confidently and respectfully advocate for themselves. This is a true citizen of the community, and one we can expect to go far in their life inside and outside of the classroom.

This type of restorative community cannot solely come from the top down, with adults asking students to meet expectations and to reflect without doing this work as a staff and by themselves. It must permeate all levels of the school with a clear unity on what the mission is. We ALL must strive to be safe, to be respectful, to be engaged and to be ourselves to achieve that mission. Adults may not meet these expectations as often as students. We must work to eliminate the shame and punishment around these instances, and maximize the safe spaces for dialogue, repairing harm, and growing through these conflicts.

How restorative language, non-evaluative language, and personal reflection on impact can include positive student actions

Non-evaluative language is a key strategy, school-wide, for two reasons. One is because of the occurrence of negative behavior, the need for non-judgmental feedback and a pause for reflection, and a connection to expectations. But this is also about positive intervention: not just making observations and asking for reflection from students not meeting expectations, but seeking the same from high-achieving students.

PRAISE VS. ENCOURAGEMENT

Courage is a movement we make in the direction to become our best selves. Encouragement is the space we make for others to find and develop their best selves. This goes beyond praise, which appears as an expression of approval or positive judgment. When we encourage others we offer a platform for empowerment and agency. Praise and encouragement can also be connected to fixed and growth mindsets.

Praise is something we give to children that feels good but that does not always assist them in personal growth. There is actually a way to give *meaningful* praise, which is encouragement. Encouragement is the space we make for others to find and develop their best selves. When we encourage others, we offer a platform for empowerment and agency.

Praise is:

You did a great job.

You did it right.

You wrote a perfect song.

I like your drawing.

Encouragement is:

I like the way you kept trying, even when things got challenging.

I know it takes bravery to share what you have been working on; what else are you planning on working on?

I noticed that you put a lot of detail into your drawing.

The difference between these two concepts can be stark but also at times very subtle. It takes work to make this switch in your daily life. We have both tried to practice this with our own children:

catching ourselves about to say, "Great job!" or "You did it!" and rephrasing into, "I love how you didn't give up and kept trying different puzzle pieces until it fit" or "I can see that you carefully put all your toys into the baskets."

Connected to this is really trying to push past generic compliments, which feel good but often don't provide much guidance to others. "You are a great singer" is nice to hear, but, "I enjoyed the times where you almost sang at a whisper, that made me emotional" gives a lot more feedback. Or, "You are a great student" is what we often want to tell a student, but how can they really digest that and use it to grow? We challenge you to simply be more specific. What makes them a great student to you? Share that. "I love how you show up and sit down five minutes before class each day" or "The questions you ask during discussions often get the whole class talking, that shows thoughtfulness." David has had this conversation on many occasions with his mother. She often used to say to his daughter that she is "such a good girl." And this, of course, is coming from a grandmother's boundless love. But he has challenged her to be more specific. Now she catches herself and says, "You are such a...no, actually, I want to say just how nice it is to see you listening to your parents and following their instructions" or "I am impressed that you can brush your teeth all by yourself," or even just replacing good with more specific words like *kind, brave, thoughtful, sweet,* or *creative.* She understands the reasoning, and although it is not what she is used to, she has almost completely made the switch and David is appreciative of her efforts to share her love in this new and restorative way!

Former places of praise can also be a chance to further practice our non-evaluative language and restorative questioning. Often if you say, "I like your drawing" the student will respond "Thanks" and the conversation is over, leaving it uncertain whether they really ever knew *why* what they'd done was good. But saying something like, "I noticed you have used a lot of blue in your drawing; tell me more about why you made that choice" will often lead to self-reflection and a deeper interaction, while also bringing the student's own sense of agency into focus. In a way, encouragement is really asking, "Tell me more about yourself, and let's look at these positive qualities together. I have noticed them and want to make sure you see them as well." This is also backed up by research by the Center for Youth Program Quality/ Weikard Center.[3]

Here is an example of replacing praise with a healthier, non-evaluative acknowledgment of behavior, in a way that a student takes objective information about their assignments and then processes it and independently realizes their successes:

Frankie, I notice that you have not missed an assignment all semester.

[Pause.]

Restorative follow-up questions can take this even further:

Destiny, Patrick and Julio, you have been in your seats on time all week.

[Pause.]

Then,

How is this impacting your classmates? What will happen if you continue to be prepared for class every day? How is your behavior impacting you and others?

Think of all the wonderful *impacts* that they may start to realize for themselves. Maybe they see that they are helping the class stay focused and on track. Maybe they see that they are sure to get a good grade if they show up prepared all year. Maybe they know that their parents will soon be happy to hear about this at parent-teacher conferences. Now they are the ones independently realizing their accomplishment and feeling an internal sense of pride, rather than simply pleasing teachers and parents. Perhaps something will even be shared that may benefit the class

---

3   See http://cypq.org

as a whole. Maybe there is something that has led to Frankie's success that can be spread across the community.

Calling out kids for doing the *right* thing can be important to remember. This is the power of noticing. Remember—as with non-evaluative statements we discussed earlier—that tone can be extremely important. There is a way to say, "Brian, you have been late three times this week" that is tinged with frustration and judgment, or it can be delivered, especially privately, in a way that is clearly calm and concerned and without personal judgment towards the student. Try out these non-evaluative statements for yourself. They can be very difficult, as we are so often used to expressing judgment, but become easier with practice.

We are preaching the value of relationships in this book. But it is not just to serve having a good time, having fun. We are driven by our genes to satisfy five basic needs: survival, love and belonging, power, freedom, and fun. For most kids the "why?" question is answered by, "Because it's fun" or "Because it's what my friends are doing" (love and belonging). Young people are driven to connect with their peers, so these motivations are completely normal and expected. Getting caught up with the "why?" question can be very distracting and unproductive. And we need to be mindful of that. So we need to focus on, "What were you hoping to achieve?" which can lead to more productive conversations. Essentially, this is not a hand-holding "everybody is best friends" methodology. It is ultimately to serve the mission: educational excellence for all. RJ is set out to achieve that, we believe, more effectively than traditional discipline strategies or behavioral modification plans, by stressing the importance of relationships and leveraging those to everyone's benefit.

In this chapter we have explored a key concept of RJ: non-evaluative statements to avoid defensiveness and shutting down conversations; restorative questions and language to encourage self-reflection and development; and using these former two to pave the way for students understanding the impact of their actions on themselves and others.

This works for both positive and negative actions in a school context. In all cases, it helps students to not just mindlessly take the praise or blame and move on, but instead to truly *understand* why the praise or blame was warranted and to learn from it going forward.

5

Shame, Empathy, Blame, and Accountability

When discussing RJ, people tend to focus on the restorative conferences that occur after a major harm has been committed. They may overlook the vast array of restorative practices and community-building activities that support these conferences and the relationships that allow them to be effective and successful. Much in the same way, people can overlook the fundamental mindset shifts that need to occur in the community. Two of the most important distinctions are between shame and empathy and between blame and accountability. That's why we have devoted a whole chapter to it! And when looking at what it takes to shift from one to the other, the answer is usually vulnerability. We, as facilitators, must be, and must teach others, how to be peaceful warriors of vulnerability.

Moving from shame towards empathy

Shame is something that we see used in schools quite often, usually with the intent of promoting better behavior in some way. But as we mentioned that you can't "punish your way into good behavior," neither can you shame your way into better behavior and stronger communities. It just doesn't work. We've all seen it happen. Think of the student who walks in late to the class and the teacher proclaims in front of the whole class, "Sandy, so nice of you to finally grace us with your presence." What a sarcastic and antagonistic thing to say. Perhaps the student was really slacking and at fault, or perhaps they just came from taking their sick sibling to the Emergency Room because no one else was available. In either case, if the student were to feel shamed and reacted by cursing at the teacher, *they* would be the one getting into trouble in most cases, not the teacher for provoking and shaming. Another great mindshift to keep in mind here is towards using non-evaluative language (see Chapter 4). This would allow you to make the observation to Sandy without sarcasm or judgement, making it known that you have noticed her absences and that you are concerned, without jumping to conclusions, being sarcastic, overtly shaming, or provoking a potential conflict.

Or consider another common example. A student is chatting during a lesson. The teacher, knowing full well that they are not paying attention, asks in front of the whole class, "Patrick, what did I just say?" The student might hang their head and slump down in their chair and shut down for the rest of the lesson. Or they may burst out in anger, which, again, they will be punished for. It is almost impossible to imagine that type of public shaming to result in a young person perking right up and suddenly engaging with the lesson. What would be a more restorative response to these cases of lateness and disengagement? Well, far be it for us to tell you how to run your class, but consider in the first case if the teacher had had a more private conversation with the student, where they showed genuine concern over why the student had been late recently, as well as concern over their grade. Imagine if they had built a relationship where the student knew that the teacher had their best interests in mind. Of course, we know that the sarcastic comments often come after numerous kind attempts to engage the student in the past—the work here is not easy. In the second example of the student talking in class, perhaps a better public comment would be, "Patrick, I really don't want you to miss this information, man." And of course it would be great to find the time for a one-on-one conversation later to better understand why the student is disengaging. But perhaps it is a recurring problem and those one-on-ones haven't worked. It might be time for a small circle of support where people who are invested in Patrick let him know that he is important and that they are all committed to his success. It is not about threatening him for talking in class with a punishment, but trying to help him to stay engaged and meet his goals. I have often used the phrase, "I'd rather be a coach than a cop" with students. And I will let them (and you) know that it is nothing against police work in general or the many honorable officers out there, just that in the school setting, I'd rather be there to work with students to do their best, than trying to catch them doing their worst.

The shift comes when you realize that shame, which is an internalized version of exclusion, does not work.

Renowned researcher and speaker Dr. Brené Brown states, "Shame is an intensely painful feeling of believing we are flawed and therefore unworthy of acceptance and belonging."[1] The idea is that "there is something intrinsically wrong with me, internally, and so I don't deserve this thing—I don't belong in this community." One of the things we can see clearly from Dr. Brown's research is that shame is toxic to feelings of belonging. This is the absolute opposite belief and experience that we want to nurture in young people. We want them to know that they belong in school, regardless of whatever the heck they did, regardless of the harm they caused—we want them to know deeply, and through our actions, that they are a valuable, important, and vibrant part of our community. And how we do that is through empathy, through nurturing experiences of connectedness or the experiences of deep and true understanding and inclusion. How we achieve that is through nurturing and normalizing vulnerability.

This is not about wallowing in guilt; it's about moving forward

Shame is different from embarrassment or guilt. What we want to make sure here is that we don't actively encourage or exacerbate

---

1   See https://brenebrown.com/blog/2013/01/14/shame-v-guilt

those negative emotions. During restorative conferences, authors of harm will undoubtedly feel some guilt or shame along with other strong emotions, which is expected when you are hearing feedback from the community. You are hearing about your mistakes, about how much work you have to do, and how you have harmed people who care about you. But we should not be actively encouraging participants to feel ashamed. And our language must be such that we are coming from a place of concern and inclusion, not out of anger and retribution. Our goal is to let them know that their actions were harmful, and also to show support and to create a safe space for them to take accountability and own those actions and participate in creating the steps needed to repair what has occurred. Shame should not be the driving force. Shame and guilt may occur, but we want to ask them to go beyond that, and not be stopped by this. We want empathy, not shame, to be the driver of the process.

The thing we are stressing here is acceptance, belonging, love, and/or inclusion. Taking such a compassionate stance can be incredibly difficult, but the idea is just so important—as is the connection of shame to long-term adult development issues. RJ aims to help build empathy, which is something that in turn really drives the restorative system forward. This is how we maintain restorative systems. The system is there to help develop the culture. The culture is made up of humans. If you follow this chain you can see that restorative systems are the practices and policies that we put in place to support a positive and successful holistic school culture. We hope to promote a system that highlights, values, and encourages our humanity. Thus, the culture will reflect a more human-oriented school culture, a culture of belonging and inclusion.

When we give detention, remove, expel, or exclude in other ways, we are telling students that they are not good enough, or valuable enough, to stay in that school community, especially when students come to us with historic experiences of exclusion, by family, country, or society. Robert Belfanz and colleagues show that even one 9th grade suspension can double the rate of dropping out of school; attending post-secondary education drops below 50 percent, and graduating on time drops 25 percent to a coin toss (50 percent).[2] It can be true that a 9th grade suspension can really be a "flag," a signal of many things. It could be a testing of the new school waters. If students didn't feel accepted or that they fit in in 6th, or 7th, or 8th grade, they may test the response of a new school. It could be a flag of trauma that is being carried, or a sense of distrust for the system. When we punitively punish, exclude, and suspend without holistic empathy and conversation, we simply confirm the student's fear that they don't belong. It reinforces shame that students already feel. We are clearly sending a message that they do not belong—and it's hard to overcome that experience. When young people make the choice to not show up at school, the hard truth is that we have failed them. We have failed to make the case that school is a place that they can and should be, and a place where they can be themselves.

So there is shame, and this relates to exclusionary discipline policies, actions that do not fulfill the five pillars of restorative justice (see Chapter 2). And then there is empathy, or connection, or feelings of belonging. What we are doing with RJ is really attempting to create systems that young people experience on a weekly, if not daily, basis, that they belong in that school, that they fit into this school and with other students, with that teacher. We have to do this really intentionally. Nicholas often says, "It is not conflict that scares us, but disconnection." When we feel disconnected, from family, peers, and school, this is where we can enter into a true sense of toxicity. And it is when students experience this sense of exclusion, and the negative feelings associated with it, that they will often act out and cause harm, if only to get attention and respect from a community they feel they are not a part of. An African proverb that we cannot recount enough times to enough people is, "The child who is not embraced

---

2   Balfanz, R., Byrnes, V. and Fox, J. (2014) "Sent home and put off track: The antecedents, disproportionalities, and consequences of being suspended in the ninth grade." *Journal of Applied Research on Children: Informing Police for Children at Risk 5*, 2. Available at: https://digitalcommons.library.tmc.edu/cgi/viewcontent.cgi?article=1217&context=childrenatrisk

by the village will burn it down to feel its warmth." Wow. We have seen this with our own eyes.

Vulnerability, courage, and empathy

Vulnerability is how we get to a space of empathy. And it is not about *telling* young people that they need to be vulnerable; it is about us being vulnerable, *modeling* that courage, and creating spaces where young people feel safe to be vulnerable with each other, to practice that skill. We have to create opportunities for a small group of young people to do this work deeply so that they can be the ambassadors who can spread this mindset and skillset. Make no mistake, this work is challenging in many ways. If you ask an educator, "When was a time where you didn't feel connected, or when you felt vulnerable?" you might find that for most folks this is a very difficult question to answer, especially in public. So if we, with all of our training and adult skills, struggle with this type of discussion, imagine how truly hard it is for a young person, sitting in a circle of peers they may already view with a lack of trust. Dr. Brown says, "Vulnerability is our most accurate measure of courage." *When it looks like courage and sounds like truth*, that is the place to which we are trying to get.

This really comes down to the level of courage that the facilitator brings to the table. We have seen examples of this courage across entire staff, schools that truly get the RJ mindset, where staff are doing restorative practices as much as they are asking students to. A great example of staff practicing vulnerability is in the sharing of "life maps" as a community-building exercise. A life map is simply a poster where you put (draw or cut out magazine images) major life events that shaped the trajectory of your life. These are turning points, often quite intense and personal, that will be shared with the group, so that they may better understand your personal journey. We were impressed by one school in particular in which the principal, who led the activity, presented his own life map, created beforehand, before asking his staff to create their own. He bravely shared deeply personal events that had made him the man he was, things like a failed relationship, the death of a loved one, as well as getting accepted into the college of his dreams. Had he not shared such personal stories (he even welled up with tears at one point speaking about them), the staff would likely also have stuck to safer waters. He could have simply shared about going to college, getting an education degree, and getting married—big events for sure, but not that revealing. By going deeper he clearly indicated that what was professionally appropriate during this activity was as wide and personal as people wanted to go, and his staff responded in spades, sharing hugely impactful and personal stories that immediately built trust and empathy within the circle. Staff shared stories of having to put parents into assisted living, battles with their teenage children, and health issues they have dealt with.

Fear begets fear, as bravery encourages risk and reward. And this is the problem with schools that ask teachers and students to engage in deeply personal and trust-building activities within the classroom, while making no space available for this within the staff's professional development or meeting time. If the culture at the top is not restorative, the system will easily collapse in on itself. By allowing staff to be and connect as whole and flawed human beings, we allow them to grow in the skills they will need to do this work with students. We want to make sure that schools are places where we can be human, where we can connect to each other, and we need to create spaces for this to occur. Sometimes we hear, "That student has got no empathy. Why are we trying RJ with him/her when they have no empathy?" We would argue that the student does not exhibit empathy because he/she might not have experienced it, and has had no model for empathy. It is our job to help students experience empathy and encourage that learning. This often means slowing down and being patient with students who have underdeveloped empathy skills. And this brings us back to daily practice—we need restorative practices to grow these skills.

We are very lucky to have had the opportunity at the NC4RJ to work with student interns. Once, the school was experiencing an issue of theft in a classroom, and they tasked the student interns with taking some restorative action to help deal with the problem. The students asked themselves, "What type of circle can we run at our school to help people realize that their actions affect other people?" And so one of the circle questions they came up with was, "When was a time you had something stolen, and how did that feel? Let's go around the class and all share a time when you have had something stolen." We have all had experience of almost every type of harm. "When was a time someone hurt you, or when someone lied to you, or cheated, or disappointed you?" We all have these experiences; whether the harm is small or large, we can connect this to our own experiences and start to build connection and empathy for others. But this is the type of discussion that does not often occur at schools, especially in the later grades of high school, and this is because we need to intentionally create space (and time) for this type of restorative discussion. We need teachers or student facilitators who feel comfortable leading these activities and discussions because they have had the chance to experience them and see how they can be done properly. And this is truly the work of RJ, creating systems and space where we can all practice talking about our problems, how they impact us, creating actionable steps to move forward after our relationships are harmed. That's empathy, that's connection, that's the work of RJ.

We frequently reference the work of Dr. Brené Brown when discussing these topics in our work with schools. Dr. Brown has many other important gems within her body of work, and one of them is worthiness—the ability to be vulnerable is connected strongly to a feeling of worthiness. "Do I feel worthy? Do I feel like I deserve good things?" So, if young people, and especially adults, do not feel worthy of something, and they end up getting it, there is shame associated with that. We have to make sure that young people are reflecting on their own sense of worthiness, and that we, as facilitators and adult guides, reflect on our own sense of worthiness. Do we feel worthy? The vast majority of us don't. We feel like we are not good enough, in some areas at least. We feel like we should be more able to control our class, we should be making more money, we should be a better parent or spouse. And it's easy to get this messaging from all around us. Even by receiving training and exploring restorative practices, it would be easy to get the feeling that we should be better teachers and, we are telling you how to do it. But this is not the case, this is not what we are saying—you are amazing human beings to choose this work, to work with young people. And the learning is simply never done; we are forever students and never masters. Our mission is to ensure that you get a space to improve this area of your craft. It is not to say that you are a bad teacher, or principal, or person because you continue to develop; there will always be space for improvement. We must be very clear in this messaging with ourselves and with our students. Some teachers and staff, when they feel that they are being told that they "need" to start "doing RJ," will have a knee-jerk reaction that they are currently doing something wrong, that they are lacking in skill. Students, when referred to RJ, can also feel this way, that they are doing something wrong and are "bad" in some way. We want the message to clearly be that "You are immensely valuable, and we love you. So much so that we want to help you to become your best self and reach your fullest potential. We are excited to see where you will grow and we believe these practices will help you be even more successful and shine in the community!" We are saying these two things at the same time when training educators—you are important as a teacher and educator, and we want to help you grow. We would never want folks to read this book and think, "Oh, I'm not a good enough teacher because I don't already do this stuff." It is all about that growth mindset, and accepting that we continue to evolve and no one amongst us is perfect.

We all share these anxieties of unworthiness, both adults and youth. We have seen these anxieties only enhanced by the rise of social media. Social media platforms are, in essence, also saying two things at the same time. They say, "Show us who you are! Share your self! Connect with others!" But then, "Only show your very best angles, filtered and scripted to make yourself appear flawless and perfect." This is hardly authentic sharing, and it affects how we interact with others in real life, in our classrooms, in our relationships, and when we look in the mirror. We must be vigilant in our affirmations of worth and belonging in order to create spaces where vulnerability is possible. Today, young people in particular struggle with how to authentically be themselves while also connecting with their peers. It might not be our job, but perhaps it is our responsibility to help young people experiment with that. We have the rare ability to create spaces where we can discuss and reflect on our being in a community. To say, "Let's sit in a circle and talk about who you really are. Let's talk about what it means to be a 7th grader and be in middle school in Seattle, or Milwaukee, or Philadelphia. What is this experience for you? What things have been hard? What do you enjoy doing? What have you struggled with? Where do you shine? What do you dream of for the future?" And let's see the connections that we share in our imperfectness. Perhaps we have a conversation about "How have you struggled with getting along with your family?" These types of questions almost always engage students as they see the rare chance to be real in a public setting and empathize with each other as they realize just how much they share in their internal worlds. And what a gift this work can be. What an amazing gift it is to let kids show each other connection and kindness as they realize that they are not alone in their hopes, their fears, their struggles, and often in their painful pasts. What a new language they will develop to describe their emotions, what perspective they will gain on the world. We honestly feel that this is as valuable as learning to divide fractions or formulate a persuasive essay.

Of course, one thought any educator may have when reading this book is, "Okay, you are asking us to prioritize relationships and to use space and time to create discussion circles and restorative activities. How in the world do I balance that with the immense pressure I feel to cover core content?" And yes, absolutely we are talking about priorities, and it may be the case that we are arguing that some of this work may be of more value to young people than certain content lessons, despite the current pressure most schools feel to deliver great results on standardized testing. But it does not have to be an "either/or." We have both seen that an investment in circle gatherings, one-on-one conversations, and restorative practices pay immense dividends as far as student engagement, attendance, and ultimately academic achievement go. We hope that slowly, this RJ movement continues to gain traction and legitimacy in schools, and is worthy of the time and effort that is carved out for it. How is it possible that practices like circle discussions could help graduation rates and academic success on mandated testing? We could give you many easy examples. One is of a past student we worked with. She was bullied at a large traditional middle school and had missed over 80 days of school in 8th grade, mostly to avoid the bullying. When she entered high school, she was involved in a safe and connected advisory community where she was able to open up and share about her experiences, hear that others had also had a hard time, and feel loved in the community, one where bullying was not accepted, not just by administration but by the student body itself. Suddenly this young girl enjoyed coming to school, missed only one day that year, and was therefore always present in her Math class, passing the state test that would certainly have been impossible if the community had been that of her previous school where she had struggled academically. This student went on to graduate on time and now works for a major company doing a job she loves. It's as simple as that sometimes—students will pass classes and improve on testing if they actually feel safe and motivated to attend school and to try. This brings the scores up quickly—it's not rocket science.

We also have to share and be vulnerable with young people and staff in a way that is professional and appropriate. This is something that can and should be discussed as a staff, as not everyone will automatically get this distinction. We feel it is okay to share some very personal things, especially with older students and other staff members if you are not going into specific details. It would be okay to say, "I have struggled to get along with some members of my family" or "I have struggled with mental health at times" or possibly even "I have struggled with addiction" or "been in an abusive relationship," depending on the group you are working with, if that was about as specific as you got in your statements. A teacher sharing with students that they have suicidal thoughts or that they are currently in an abusive relationship isn't appropriate sharing, because it would be scary and place an unfair burden on students who would want to take action. We are also very clear with students before any of these sharing conversations as to what exactly our roles are as mandated reporters. That it is our job and our responsibility as educators to report instances where we think someone will be or is being harmed or harming others. We are always open to discuss what this means and what exactly we would be obligated to share. Transparency is important, and all educators should be clear themselves about what must be reported and what can be kept confidential. To recap: (1) don't go into specific details or (2) share in a way where it is absolutely clear that you are not asking for or implying that you need help. These are two important rules to keep in mind.

With those caveats, it is important to note how powerful these vulnerable shares can be, and why they should not be shied away from. David remembers early in his teaching career mentioning to his class that he would be absent for two days, and for no particular reason, explaining that it was because his grandmother had passed away. After class that day, a student he often had troubles with in the classroom came up to him and said, "Sorry about your grandma, I lost mine too last year, that's really tough." And he gave a half-hug. This was easily the best interaction he had had with this student thus far. David realized that he could have easily not mentioned why he would be absent, as teachers often don't share these things, but how being authentic and sharing a small part of his out-of-classroom struggles had connected him with at least that one student in a deeper way. This was a light-bulb moment.

Another example we heard was from a teacher who was struggling to get his class to really open up and engage in class discussions. This 9th grade teacher wrote in a journal, as he asked all students to on Monday mornings, and one day he found himself writing about his desire to start a small beer brewing company as a hobby, but also wondering if it would be appropriate for someone who works with minors to also sell alcohol. He decided, hesitantly, to share the journal entry with his class. He could not believe how every student was listening to him read, and soon began vigorously discussing and debating his possible business from all angles. He had shared rather safe and guarded entries before and had never had that positive discussion experience.

Nicholas shares a story of a woman who worked in a middle school who experienced the death of her husband, and after building a deep classroom sharing environment was able to share this with her students. Not only did they demonstrate kindness and concern, many of them also opened up throughout the year about people they had lost and how that had made them feel. She had modeled what it looks like to bravely deal with grief and loss while trusting your community to be kind. Those students benefited from that relationship. As hard and as scary as it is, we must not shy away from major impactful events that have happened in our students' lives, whether it is something local, like the loss of a teacher, or something more removed but impactful, like a school shooting in another state. It is not about being a counselor; you would be right to feel unqualified to assume that role as a classroom teacher. It is simply about asking real questions, and allowing students to speak and listen to each other. "How are you feeling about Ms Jackson being gone?" "When you heard of the recent school shooting, how did you feel?" In most instances, as facilitators, we can simply say, "thank you all for sharing," after the group members have all had a chance to speak. We are not giving advice or adding our own opinions; just teaching the skill of pausing to reflect and valuing others' experiences. We are not looking to solve students' problems for them; just offering compassion and a space for listening and support, where all members can practice being vulnerable without shame.

Moving from blame towards accountability

We live in a society where we are taught to never admit fault, to avoid taking accountability. In court, people often plead "not guilty" even when they are obviously guilty, in the hope of escaping punishment. (Ironically, people also often plead "guilty" when they are innocent in a plea deal to reduce their punishment.) We are taught that when you get into a car accident not to apologize, because that would imply you were at fault and you could be liable for damages. When we make a mistake at work, we look for excuses and others to blame. And yet, in schools, we want students to own up to their mistakes and immediately take responsibility. Talk about unrealistic expectations. Kids learn from us and we are, as a society, horrible about taking accountability. This is something that must be taught and learned and practiced within a restorative system.

It feels so good to blame others, because it takes us out of the hot seat ourselves. We would rather blame someone than have no one to blame. Blame is toxic; it gets in our way of connecting, accountability, etc. We need to make sure that we are moving away from blame.

Shifting responsibility can be as gratifying as scratching an itch or hitting snooze on the alarm and sleeping in. It is human nature and yet, when trying to resolve conflicts, it really gets us nowhere. Take the example of a student who is really struggling to pass almost any classes or meet grade-level expectations. You can easily imagine the "blame game" occurring here. Parents might think it's the teacher's fault; teachers may think the parents aren't doing enough or that school admin is not providing enough support. School admin might feel restricted by the superintendent or school district demands on the school. Everyone, we can assume, shares the exact same wish—that the student was more successful in school—and their time and energy is spent blaming others, with no positive result. And yet, this is how we live our lives. The fact is, that blame is often not helpful in resolving conflict. Accountability is the antidote to blame. We would like to write that one more time: *accountability is the antidote to blame.* And here is a concept that we really want to make clear as well. You cannot actually hold someone else accountable; you can only create an environment where they feel safe to take accountability for their own actions.

This is counter to the common statement you will hear in cases of discipline in schools and in the criminal system: "He/she must be held accountable!" It is through detentions and suspensions (or prison sentences) that folks often think they are holding someone else accountable. Consider this: you can blame others, but you can only truly hold yourself accountable.

Let's return to our example. The teacher, parents, administrators—all pointing a finger at others for the student's lack of success. Imagine if instead of spending all their time blaming, these folks gathered in a circle to each help take accountability and control of the situation, to pledge an action on behalf of the student, and the student being part of that circle, also taking ownership and making plans to take action. Imagine all these stakeholders working and supporting each other in this goal of literacy—it is hard to imagine that the student would not make great progress towards this goal quickly.

Owning up to a major act of harm is incredibly hard, for students and adults alike. We must create spaces where people can feel comfortable to take accountability, to feel remorse, and yet know that they are still wanted in the community. If we practice this often (see "Accountability circles" in Chapter 10), with lower-level issues, it is easier to do it in times of major crisis.

All of this goes back to issues of agency and empowerment. Through learning about impact, students can begin to see how their actions can negatively affect themselves and those around them. This is what we often want in the discipline process. But it is important not to miss the other side of the coin, that we also hold the power to positively affect our community. We all want to feel powerful and not powerless. When we blame others, we make ourselves powerless ("I can't make other people pick up their blocks"). When we practice accountability, we feel empowered ("I could have raced my friends to see who could pick up the most blocks the fastest. That would have been fun and would have helped make the class clean!").

This plays out particularly well when mediating conflict. Imagine a situation where a student is being bullied for having big eyes. Students are teasing her over this. And in particular, they are walking up to her and opening their eyes as wide as possible and laughing. Imagine this girl gets fed up with the teasing and shoves someone taunting her in this way onto the ground and they get hurt. In a traditional discipline system, in most cases, the girl being teased would be punished. The girl who provoked may claim, "You can't punish me just for opening my eyes!" And she would seem to be right. But if we shift away from who we can or cannot punish towards taking accountability, we can make breakthroughs. We can hold a circle where the girl being teased can feel empowered to share what she is going through personally as a result of being bullied, where other students can own their antagonizing behavior, where staff can even jump in, perhaps owning that they were not aware enough as to what was going on. Perhaps everyone shares a time that they were teased or bullied and how that made them feel, thus building empathy. Now the issue has been brought to light, a learning moment is not lost to denial and blame, and the community is now monitoring it from all sides with many eyes to make sure it does not continue—it is hard for bullying to remain when exposed to the light. A later check-in circle could be convened to see how the issue is going, and to provide positive feedback where it is due.

THE POWER OF VULNERABILITY

Two days ago, in Ms T's first period 11th grade classroom, there had been an incident between two female students, Shannon and Aida. Ms T felt like the matter could be resolved in a circle mediation, which she asked me to facilitate. Two days later, both girls were in school, so we quickly jumped on the opportunity, getting another teacher to cover the class so that we could all meet in a private room. In addition to Ms T, myself, and the two students, we had also invited Andy, the school social worker/counselor, because he had a good working relationship with both girls.

The five of us sat around the small table and began by

establishing what had happened. Shannon began, "Well I was coming to English and I was late. I'll admit I haven't been to that class much this year. I've got some stuff going on at home. I just knew that when I walked in to class someone was gonna say something smart or give me a look. And sure enough, this girl right here had to make some slick comment like 'Is she even in this class?' And then her smart ass friends had to laugh so I got tight [upset] and we exchanged words. That's it."

"Okay," I said, "thank you for your perspective. Aida, is that how you saw things happen?"

"Look, all I know is that Shannon came into the class mad late, so I turned around like everyone else to see who it was. I haven't seen her in my class before so, yeah, without thinking on it, I did say that comment. I didn't mean it to be a diss, and I didn't know kids were gonna laugh at it. But then she says something about me wiping the look off my ugly face and no one talks to me like that, especially not in front of all those people, so I fired back."

"Thank you for sharing, Aida. I can see Shannon nodding and saying 'yes,' she agrees with what you said. Aida, now that we are here, is there anything you can take responsibility for in that exchange?"

"Yeah, I really didn't need to make that comment. I was surprised to see her but I should have just kept that to myself. Especially now that I heard she's going through something at home, she probably didn't need any more stress from me."

"Thank you Aida. Shannon, is there anything you can take responsibility for now that we are here and calm?"

"Yeah, I guess I was already on edge, and I can understand that she was surprised to see me there. I've just been trying to get back on my school game. Anyway, I was pissed but I shouldn't have insulted her and almost got into a fight. That didn't help anything."

"You girls are both such strong and wonderful students," Ms T added, "I hate to see you fight like that and tear each other down."

Shannon and Aida both nodded. "We love you Ms T and sorry for messing up your class like that," offered Shannon.

I could see that the issue was adequately resolved at this

point and that the mood of the circle had shifted towards something more safe and supportive. Not entirely sure why, as I had not planned to do this, I decided to add something else to this mediation, something that would push us further into vulnerability and empathy, two aspects of RJ that can often be overlooked.

"You know, Ms T has told me about how wonderful you two are, and also that you both have had struggles in your life. I really want to acknowledge the strength it takes to keep working at school despite what's going on for you outside. So I'd like to finish this meeting with one request, that we each share one struggle we have had in our life. Something you feel comfortable sharing, and I want to be clear that nothing said here leaves this room. Can we agree to that? Good. I know it's hard, so I will go first. Hmm, let's see. Well, many years ago I was diagnosed with anxiety and depression. It got so bad that I had to get the help of a psychologist, a counselor like Andy, and even go on some medication. I feel much better these days but I went through a really dark time, especially in my 20s dealing with how badly I felt. Thank you for listening. Shannon, would you share something?"

"Okay, well yeah, like I was saying, I've been missing a lot of school. I live with my grandma, she is the one who raised me. And she got really sick this year, it might be cancer. So I've had to stay home a lot and look after my younger brother and sister. If something happens to her, I just don't know what I'm gonna do."

"Thank you for sharing that Shannon, that sounds really scary."

"Yeah, damn. Hearing all that, now I really feel bad that I made that comment," Aida interjected. "I hope things get better for your grandma."

"Thanks."

"Andy, you've been a very good listener through all this, is there something you could share that you've been through?" I asked.

"Okay, well sure," Andy began. "I recently broke up with my

boyfriend. We were living together and so, yeah, that was really hard."

I didn't know what to expect from the other adults in the circle and I really appreciated the personal share from Andy. I wasn't sure if the two girls were aware that he was gay, but either way, he showed vulnerability with his share and the two girls said some words of encouragement to him.

"Aida, it's your turn, if you would share something with us," I requested.

"Okay, yeah well. One thing I struggled with was not knowing my father. He left my mom and I when I was just a baby. Sometimes when I think about it I get really angry, like I wish he was there for me all these years, so I try not to think on it that much."

"We hear you. Those sound like really tough thoughts to have, and we thank you for sharing. Last, but not least, Ms T, would you mind sharing with the group?"

"Well, as you girls know, I grew up right around here. And you also know how important it is in New York, when you're young, to have the latest sneakers and look fresh in school. But my family was really poor. It was just my mom taking care of me and my brothers. So every year I would get one pair of white [Nike] Air Force 1s, and they had to last me the whole year. I would..."

At this point Ms T got emotional and began wiping tears from her eyes. Aida put a comforting hand on her shoulder.

"Sorry, I'm okay," Ms T. continued. "I would use a toothbrush to clean the shoes all the time, hoping that none of the other kids would notice that I didn't get any new shoes. So they wouldn't know how poor my family was."

Now Shannon also put a hand on Ms T's shoulder.

"Thank you. I want to acknowledge the powerful sharing you all just did here in this circle. A reminder not to jump so quickly into anger with other people when we never really know what's going on in their lives that might be affecting them. Shannon and Aida, I wish you the best in your classes this semester, you are lucky to have such a caring teacher as Ms T wanting the best for you. All of us at this table are here if you ever need to talk to someone about any struggles you are having."

Story debrief

This last part of the mediation, sharing our own vulnerabilities, was not planned, but it felt right for the girls to be acknowledged for the difficulties they have been experiencing and the strength they were showing to persevere. It was also valuable for them to hear that Ms T, a young teacher from their own neighborhood, had experienced struggles as well, and was still able to achieve a college degree and a successful career. This is the type of work that can strengthen relationships between students and staff, the type of authentic connection that would not have occurred if the girls were simply written up for detention, where they would sit in silence without the opportunity for this type of personal and compassionate dialogue. Vulnerability is rarely valued or modeled with young people in our schools. Vulnerability can often be equated with weakness, but if anything, this exercise allowed the girls' true strength to shine.

6

Cultural Competency

BIAS, CURIOSITY, INSTITUTIONAL RACISM

Cultural competency is incredibly important to RJ. Without cultural competency we cannot begin to understand the many different types of communication and experiences that exist around us. We also cannot find common ground on the challenging issues of race and equity that affect us all, particularly members of marginalized groups struggling for fair treatment in schools and society at large. A high level of cultural competency is required to create and maintain strong relationships and connections. RJ is the relational approach to conflict, and the success of the work depends a great deal on how we navigate the intersections of culture, privilege, and power. In short, cultural competency is essential for good communication, communication is the number one skill for building relationships, and relationships predict success in schools. Clearly, therefore, this is something that is very important to discuss and be aware of.

A somewhat bulky definition of cultural competency is: a set of congruent behaviors, attitudes, and policies that come together in a system, agency, or amongst professionals, that enable that system, agency, or those professionals to work effectively in cross-cultural situations.

Basically, we want our communities to work collaboratively, harmoniously, and effectively while embracing (not in spite of) our diverse cultural backgrounds.

We understand conversations around race and privilege can be extremely divisive and difficult, and so many people prefer to steer clear of them entirely. And for those of us who get classified into groups of privilege, such as *white, male, heterosexual, cisgender,* or *able-bodied*, it is much easier to simply avoid this topic altogether as educators, despite the fact that many of our students and some of our staff may, on a daily basis, be struggling against inequity and injustice due to their culture. Being able to ignore the topic of culture is part of privilege, or of being of the dominant culture. And because those with power and authority, in schools and elsewhere, disproportionately come from these privileged groups, this topic is not adequately dealt with between staff or students in most schools across the country.

Depending on how much issues of race impact your daily lives, this may form an indispensable part of how you process the world around you. For folks who often encounter issues of race, it can be impossible to imagine navigating the world without considering the impact of race. And yet, for someone who is rarely forced to think about their race (in America this is often white folks) it can be equally unimaginable to see almost every social situation as impacted by factors of race. Without building empathy (see Chapter 5), we can suffer a great deal of misunderstanding and conflict within our communities.

Culture has power, and we make meaning from culture. Our whole worldview is shaped by our cultural lens. Understanding this goes a long way towards having empathy and understanding for each other. If our goal is to promote relationships while in peace and in conflict, we have to have these conversations about culture and what that word means. For instance, let's say you do or don't get a job. One person may say that it's because they simply didn't have the right qualifications, where another may think it was due in part to their race, or because they have a felony, or because she is a woman applying in a predominantly male field. As so many aspects of prejudice and bias are unconscious, it can be difficult to ever really know the truth. What we do know with certainty is that there exist many toxic, and absolutely false, paradigms that are pervasive in our society.

These include, but are not limited to:

- Heterosexuals are more deserving of love than homosexuals.

- Light-skinned people are more deserving of respect than darker-skinned people.

Unchecked, these ideas become the water that we swim in. And often the groups that benefit the most from these biases are those with the most power to change them. And so they continue and become entrenched. Our work must be to uncover and confront these harmful ideas that lurk in ourselves and in our communities.

While this work we do is designed to illuminate and transform systemic racism, it is also about valuing human relationships. We are human, so how do we support people in building relationships across cultural subsets?

We believe it is the responsibility of those in power to unmake unjust systems—it's not the role of young people to solve these issues for adults or the country at large, although young people are absolutely valuable and wholly worthy of inclusion in the dialogue and actions taking place.

There is a fear, especially by those in power who most often carry privileges, even those folks with the best intentions who care deeply about their staff and students, that they might say the wrong thing. There is a culture of "rightness" that makes us feel we can only say what has been unanimously approved and is not controversial. Although being thoughtful and aware in conversations around race is essential, this idea of being right or wrong can really get in the way of us connecting authentically as humans.

Our belief is that we are better as a community when we are together. And when groups are excluded or negatively impacted, this harms us as a whole, even those with privilege. When one suffers in the community, we all suffer. And so we must have these conversations, which can actually be delightful and enlightening, so let's dive in!

Quick insight: In our trainings we have had several instances of knee-jerk reactions, defensiveness, and push-back against the concept of "white privilege." For a lot of white folks, this can be where they immediately shut down and tune out. You will commonly hear someone say something in the realm of, "Hey, I'm white, and I had an extremely hard life. We were on food stamps and I had to work my way through school. Nobody gave me anything. I find it offensive that you are saying I'm privileged." This somewhat understandable response only highlights the need for some simple clarification, and it really is simple—when we talk of "white privilege," we are not saying that if you are white you must have had an easy life. We are only saying that the color of your skin has *not* made your life harder.

So what is culture? For our purposes we will define it as: the intersection of one's national origin, religion, language, sexual orientation, socio-economic class, age, gender identity, race, ethnicity, and physical/developmental ability. These are 10 classifications that can greatly affect people's lives, how they are treated, how they treat others, and that shape the lens through which the entire world is viewed. Especially when people wield power, being unaware of these experiences and perceptions can lead to great inequity, bias, and harm in school communities. We see this in the disproportionate discipline and incarceration of certain groups as a prime and tragic example.

People often try to put culture in a box, but culture is an immensely personal experience, one that is a result of the infinite combinations of these aspects of culture that intersect for us all. It is profoundly ignorant to make assumptions about someone's experience based on their perceived culture, race, etc. We must be in conversation with that person to better understand.

We also know and want to recognize that race is a social construct, an arbitrary classification drawn between different groups, historically used to "justify" the oppression and exploitation of Africans and other black and brown bodies around the world. We are one human race, of course, despite these divisions used to subjugate and harm. And yet we also know and see the *very real* impacts of race, racism, and culture on our communities and folks of color specifically. We see the disproportionality in discipline in schools; we see the economic gap between men and women, whites and non-whites. We see the difference in quality of schools and resources in affluent communities to those that serve lower-income families. There are countless ways in which racism in our society causes real harm and must be addressed.

Now is a good time to give a few helpful definitions:

- **Racism:** the belief that members of each race possess characteristics that distinguish it as inferior or superior to other races.

- **Structural racism:** society has been structured in a way that excludes substantial numbers of people of color from taking part in social institutions equally.

- **Institutional racism:** systems of inequality based on race that occur within institutions such as public government bodies and private business corporations.

- **Implicit bias:** attitudes or stereotypes that affect our understanding, actions, and decisions in an unconscious manner.

- **Discrimination:** the use of power positions to disempower those different from oneself.

Perhaps you might be feeling some apprehension around addressing this topic in your school. This is quite normal, and yet we must not shy away, especially those of us who hold privilege and power in our schools and society. Remember, it is not about being right. You don't have to feel guilty or wrong simply because you are white or because you are a straight man, for instance, or because you have no major physical disability. We just all need to engage in this work humbly and courageously and with personal awareness.

It helps us to be brave when we think of it this way: we are striving for cultural *competency*, not cultural *mastery*. This work, like teaching in general, is an art form, a practice in which you can always be reflecting on and improving. We don't need to be perfect here, just aware. We are going to share with you two HUGE secrets to success, from our RJ trainings on this topic, the only tools you need to be culturally competent and engage in these difficult discussions around race, culture, and privilege. If you only take away two things from this chapter, we hope that it will be:

The keys to cultural competency are to be respectfully curious and to do your own work.

Let's look closer at this:

- *Be respectfully curious:* this means that when engaging with someone around their race or culture, come from a place of genuine listening. Forget about your own previously held assumptions or experiences with their culture, and value what they have to share. This is about asking questions, and also simply following someone's lead, waiting to have a strong relationship before posing a personal or potentially invasive question. It is about being aware and kind and coming from a place of seeking only to better understand someone you care about.

- *Do your own work*—and this is so important: this simply means spending time uncovering your own culture, the struggles and privileges that have come along with it, to unpack your own life experiences and how they have shaped your view of others. This is especially important for those who enjoy the most privileges and power. It is dangerous to knowingly or unknowingly walk around feeling or thinking that your culture is "normal" and that others are foreign, or different, or less important.

We have done a lot of training on cultural competency, practicing these two simple strategies in groups, working in particular on growing our understanding of our own cultural roots, our own privileges, and our own cultural experiences. There are several activities that you can utilize to grow your community of staff and students in cultural competency, and we will share some questions that can be useful in this exploration:

- *Choose one of the 10 aspects of your culture from the list mentioned above, and explain what you consider to be an important part of that culture.* Remember that this is from your perspective—there are no right or wrong answers, and two people of the same culture may not agree...and that's okay! It's your experience of your own culture. Listening to and valuing everyone's answers is part of "respectful curiosity."

  Adult groups usually have no trouble with this activity. You have heard things like, "As a woman [gender] I think taking care of family is really valued." "As an American [country of origin] I see that sports and cars are very popular parts of the culture." The answers can range from light and funny to deep and personal. Younger students can have these conversations too, but may need more modeling and explanation.

- *Choose one aspect of culture from the list of 10 that you don't normally think about, and share how it has affected your life and experiences.* Commonly, we get a lot of folks reflecting on being able-bodied, as many of us are of this group and do not have to think about it. It is a privilege to make plans to go to a restaurant, or theater, or a school building, and not have to be concerned about whether there are stairs to navigate if you have a limited mobility, for instance. Age is another from the list that often turns up in these discussions. These reflections are great for gaining awareness of "blindspots," aspects of culture and privileges that impact your life often without much notice, even for folks who might not feel they enjoy privilege in other areas of their culture.

- *What is one assumption that you do not want people to make about you based on your culture?* This is a place where people can confront stereotypes and present themselves more authentically.

- *What does it mean to be [list one aspect of your culture], or [slight variation]? What does it mean to be [list one aspect of your culture] in America?* This is an extremely powerful and complex discussion that allows people to reflect on their personal experiences through one specific lens, and to share the impact of those moments with others, to help them gain understanding, from the outside, as to what it might mean to be lesbian, or Chinese, or a woman, or Hindu in America. These can be fascinating insights.

It is important to note that these discussions can only happen safely and authentically after building strong relationships and trust. We would never advise asking someone out of the blue to explain what it means to be black in America, or what it means to be Muslim. It is not someone's job to educate us on their culture simply because we ask them to, not to mention that these questions might be quite invasive and off-putting without relationships at the base. This is why RJ is all about starting with building strong and safe bonds. Just because you have worked with staff members or students for several years, this does not guarantee that trust is there. You have to actively build it. But if you do and you demonstrate honest and respectful curiosity, you just may learn a great deal about the lives of those around you. Last, but not least, do the work yourself. If you are fortunate enough for someone to share with you some of their personal cultural experiences, you will be better prepared (having earnestly reflected on this previously) and willing to share if they ask you in return to share what it means to be a person with your cultural background.

If you are wondering what it might be like to be a black man in America, or a woman, gay, or Hindu, or differently abled, or a senior citizen, because you have not had those experiences, and because you want to increase your empathy and understanding of those in your community, that is a good thing. It means that you are respectfully curious! Just remember, especially if you are from one or more of the privileged groups, and particularly if you hold a position of power and authority, to be aware of how you are requesting this information from others. A great idea is to build safe and strong relationships around less intense topics, through community-building circles and experiences, and then try some of the discussion questions above. These are great ways to approach the topic, to learn about others' experiences, and to share your own, without being invasive, or off-putting, or exacerbating a sense of inequity that may already exist in the space. And, of course (and we can't say this enough), do your own work to unpack what it means for you to carry cultural privilege and to hold a position of power amongst those who may not. If you, as a facilitator, are concerned about the power dynamics in this type of discussion, you can always openly take those concerns back to the group. You could ask the circle to answer "How do you feel about me asking these questions about culture today?" Hearing how people feel about the activity can also be enlightening.

Implicit bias

Implicit bias means attitudes or stereotypes that affect our understanding, actions, and decisions in an unconscious manner.

In addition to uncovering your own culture, privilege, and experiences, discovering your implicit biases is another great way to "do your own work." But, like *white privilege*, *bias* is a term that can immediately get a knee-jerk reaction. For instance, you might hear someone say: "I'm not biased. Yes, I am white, but I have dedicated my life to serving students of color and I treat everyone equally." The key clarification here is that implicit bias is something that occurs *unconsciously*, unintentionally, and without our control. It is interesting to note that almost every single person carries biases of which they may not be aware, and some biases can be counter-intuitive on the surface. For instance, research at Harvard has shown that the vast majority of us have at least a mild bias towards non-marginalized or privileged societal groups.[1] This includes African-American, black, and Hispanic people. This seems mind-boggling until you look at how people of color are widely portrayed in the news, movies, and across pop culture. We have all been shown countless mugshots of black men on television news, for instance, perhaps more than we have been shown images of successful, influential, and happy black men. Our minds have been populated by these representations. So when someone says "thug," the image that pops into our minds has been crafted by years of people of color being portrayed this way in the news, television and movies. And usually this internal image is different from what we might imagine when we hear "corporate CEO." These mental leaps happening without our intention can also influence our day-to-day interactions and expectations of others based solely on how they look or sound, especially if unchecked.

For our RJ courses at the NC4RJ, we use the Project Implicit bias online test from Harvard.[2] This asks us to sort and match images and words (both positive and negative), and then to interpret our response times. The idea is that the sorting that goes against our immediate internal bias will take longer to complete. For example, if you are taking a test to determine gender or career bias, you will be asked to sort male and female names and other words that relate to career or family as fast as possible. Many people will discover that they are naturally able to sort male identity with career and female identity with family faster. This would show some bias towards male/career and female/family. There are many categories that you can test, including your response

---

1   See https://implicit.harvard.edu/implicit/faqs.html#faq1o
2   See https://implicit.harvard.edu/implicit/takeatest.html

to race, sexuality, age, religion, and disability. It can be troubling to receive the results from these tests, however, especially when we show unconscious bias towards a group that we serve in our career and genuinely care about, or because we have daughters we want to treat fairly, or just because we don't wish to be a biased person. The fact is, we all carry some bias towards those of us who look, think, and act like ourselves. This is human nature. This is why in any teacher lounge you will often see people sitting with others who look, act, and think like they do, and often people group into those of similar age. This is not always the case, but it happens to some degree universally. The test results can feel embarrassing, shameful, and wrong. The results may make you angry. This is totally normal, as we all want to be the best for *all* students, regardless of race. And yet this work is about moving from shame to empathy. So understanding that a lifetime in the USA (and other countries, of course), where we have a history of racism and biased images, has a powerful effect on our deep consciousness. So many of us have been "poisoned" in this way and it is normal for implicit bias to be the result. The important thing is not to stop there, to bury our heads or run away from this topic, but to acknowledge that we need to stay humble and vigilant and watch for these slight biases as they might creep into our work or our dispensation of discipline, and to look for ways to ensure equity. We believe that RJ is one tool to increase equity.

These bias tests are obviously quick, and their effectiveness or reliability has been queried.[3] We are complex individuals with multifaceted personalities that cannot be distilled in 3–5 minutes. But it is unarguable that our performance on these tests clearly illuminates discrepancies that we carry when categorizing types of people with certain concepts. In our opinion, the effect these tests can have is to illuminate the fact that even the most well-intentioned person may still carry implicit bias, and to simply ignore this fact would be detrimental to our work as RJ facilitators

---

3   Lopez, G. (2017) "For years, this popular test measured anyone's racial bias. But it might not work after all." Vox, March 7. Available at: www.vox.com/identities/2017/3/7/14637626/implicit-association-test-racism

and educators. So what to do with this new and uncomfortable information?

In one of our RJ training sessions with the NC4RJ, someone mentioned that they had an upcoming meeting to discuss an academically struggling student. Both the student and the mother are African American and they would be meeting with three white women from the school staff. They asked: "Should the race/power dynamic be addressed directly?" This was a *great* question. We would say, as a practice, not to awkwardly lead with this discussion. After all, the meeting is not supposed to be about race at all. But we think it is *wonderful* that this race/power dynamic is on this person's mind as a facilitator. She had even tried to empathize, and thought, "What if it were me sitting across from three men in power? I might feel intimidated." This is a fantastic example of trying to put yourself into someone else's shoes to build empathy. We would suggest, first, to look for ways to make the circle more equitable and comfortable. We would never advocate dragging another staff member into the circle simply because they were African American, like the family. But *do* look for staff with authentic connections to the family and their community that would make sense in the circle. In one school we often invited the parent-teacher coordinator to some of the facilitated circles. She was a woman who not only looked like many of the students; she had also grown up in the local neighborhood and had deep connections in the community. She was also a mother of a young black man and her words had *huge* power in those circles. It made sense for her to be there. So, know the diversity on your staff and look to increase it in your circles, where authentic. At times, race may also come up organically. I've had students say something like, "Mr J doesn't like me because I'm black." That is a case where we might ask, "Okay, we can discuss this, but how do you feel having me lead the circle, when I am white? Is there someone else you would like us to invite to this discussion as well?" Usually just acknowledging the dynamics at play and making space for adjustment is enough to increase a sense of trust and comfort for the student. Despite how legitimate you feel their claim of racism might be, it is important that the student feels heard and not immediately dismissed. So, race in this context of that upcoming parent meeting may not need to be addressed outright, but having it in your mind and being aware of it can often lead to better, more equitable, and more successful, facilitation.

David shares that sometimes he has addressed race/power directly with students: "How do you guys feel about me being the teacher and also the only 'white guy' in the room?" It is important to note that this comes after a *lot* of community building and often organically when his group is already having a talk on race, not something that comes out of nowhere in a space that has not yet established safety. But if you do the groundwork, you *can* have these powerful conversations.

Specifically, on one occasion during a frank conversation with a group that already had strong relationships, he posed similarly: "I notice I am the only white guy in the room, and I am the one teaching. What is that like for you?" A talking piece was passed around the gathered circle to share and listen. Notably there were several students who stated the same thing, "It's like that in a lot of my classes, so I'm used to it." Another interesting share was from a young woman in the class, "They call me African American but I was born here, so I don't like that term, I don't feel connected to Africa." This really stuck with David because the general consensus would be that African American would be the right/correct (there it is again!) term to describe this student's race. But here she was, after actually being asked, expressing her individual perspective and feelings about the label. David was also allowed to share his feelings about the label "white" and what it was like to be the "white guy in the room." Conversations like this rarely get to happen in a classroom. Experiences like this will make you realize that it can be safe to have open discussions if you do not have an agenda, and are vulnerable and respectful in your approach. You may also realize that assumptions are dangerous, such as assuming the term African American will be preferred by everyone in the group.

In our NC4RJ courses we often discuss how feasible it might be to have these types of conversations about race in the participants' schools, what might be some obstacles to this occurring safely, and what might be needed to create space for these conversations.

Awareness of implicit bias is a huge part of the work. A white teacher walking into a culturally diverse classroom believing "I have no bias" is actually more dangerous than walking in as a teacher who has identified an implicit bias and is careful to be aware of their actions and decisions in the classroom to ensure equity. This might help us to ensure that we are not unintentionally calling on certain students, giving out coveted responsibilities to certain students, and especially aware of how we are disciplining different students for the same infractions or harm. Having a system of measures and accountability in place is a great way to generate data that can illuminate potential bias.

"Doing the work" can be incredibly uncomfortable, as it might mean acknowledging privilege and/or bias that has shaped our experience of the world. But we simply cannot create equitable systems, especially as those in power, without wielding this knowledge and constantly working to check our bias and privilege as it presents itself.

Culture is to be acknowledged, celebrated, and respected. However, cultural aspects that divide us are problematic. If a student wants to be separate because they are homophobic, religiously bigoted, or racist, we simply cannot abide by those requests. These are issues that must be dealt with directly, with care and with collaboration.

Cultural competency will often mean navigating troubled waters and finding balance, engaging in discussion with folks and being humble, caring, and thoughtful. It means keeping your core principles and beliefs at heart, but also looking for ways to collaborate and evolve.

A teacher who is not African American or Latino may hear the plea, "Make your classroom more welcoming to students of color." They may genuinely make attempts. They might decide to start the day by attempting a motivating rap to the class, thinking that students of color would enjoy this. They might then hear,

"No, not like that! Don't use their culture in that way. That's not appropriate or correct!" It can be confusing and difficult for some to figure out how to accomplish the goal of creating welcoming spaces. Keep this in mind: the more we can be aware of how we impact others, the better. We, as humans, generally speaking, have a difficult time seeing how we negatively impact others. But what is even more challenging is noticing when we impact folks from other cultural groups. Asking your class or community how the space could be more welcoming, or asking for feedback on your ideas and initiatives to accomplish this goal, would be a great place to start.

So what are we asking for? Cultures change, grow, and evolve over time, and individuals experience cultures differently, even within largely the same cultural groups. From an RJ perspective we want to make sure we are noticing the impact our actions have on others, and the goal should always be to have more of a positive than a negative impact. It is that simple, and it will never be perfect. This means we will hurt people—not *if* we do, but *when* we do, we need to take accountability. If the students in our school or class have an issue with the way we invite them into the classroom, we need to hear that. We need to be asking the group for honest feedback in listening circles. The balance we are seeking may mean allowing space for historically disempowered groups, perhaps where they might gather exclusively in clubs or activities. How can we accomplish this conscious separation while still maintaining a culture of inclusion and belonging? These are the types of questions we need to ask of the community, not simply trying to decide for others at an administrative level. Of course, dialogue and discussion takes valuable time, but discord and conflict as a result of ignoring cross-cultural issues takes even more.

WATERMELON

At the end of a long week of classes, a 10th grade girl from the student government was standing on stage, making her announcement over the buzz of 300 students gathered in our high school auditorium for the assembly. As she finished talking, she looked up with a smile and passed the microphone to another student council member standing to her left. He quickly jumped forward with energy and confidence and asked the crowd if they were "ready for the fun part of the assembly?!" This was the tradition at our school; the all-school assemblies were organized and hosted by the student government, with staff members adding important announcements and highlighting community achievements. The events usually ended with some sort of fun performance or game to pick up everyone's spirits before heading home for the weekend.

For this day's entertainment, there were four desks set up side by side on the stage, and the young man holding the mic was asking for one volunteer from each grade level (9, 10, 11, 12) to "come up and compete." A cacophony of yelling and hand waving erupted from the crowd as he slowly picked out four students who each walked up on stage to take seats at the tables. Helpers from the student government brought out giant slices of watermelon and placed them in front of each contestant, for the "Minute to win it watermelon eating contest!" This type of game was pretty typical of what we often had—there had been a pie eating contest in the fall, for example. But as the host yelled "Go!" and the students began furiously devouring the slices of wet, pink watermelon, something immediately felt off. It is well known that after emancipation, watermelon was used by southern whites as a derogatory symbol associated with freed black slaves.[4] As I watched one of our darkest skinned students, up on stage, in front of a hooting and hollering crowd, digging into the watermelon, my eyes flitted quickly and uncomfortably around the auditorium. I locked eyes with a fellow staff member and I could tell that she was in disbelief. Almost everyone in the auditorium was having fun and cheering, however, and I didn't see or hear anyone being

4 Black, W.R. (2014) "How Watermelons Became a Racist Trope." *The Atlantic*. December 8. Available at: https://www.theatlantic.com/national/archive/2014/12/how-watermelons-became-a-racist-trope/383529.

offensive to the students on stage. But my concern that this may negatively impact some students was confirmed when a senior I knew well looked at me with a shocked expression as she mouthed the words, "What the hell?"

It all happened so quickly that I didn't react. As a white ally, I felt a strong urge to stop the event, as it was clearly an inappropriate display of racialized imagery with no place in a public school, regardless of how many others may not be aware of the historical or systematic harm to which it was attached. All I could do in the moment was stand in shock with my mouth open and then help the students file out from the auditorium. Following the assembly we had a staff meeting, and, during our brief break before the meeting, I talked with a fellow teacher in my classroom about the spectacle. We wondered how this had happened and what needed to happen next.

At the staff meeting, one of the African-American teachers stood up pretty quickly and proclaimed, "I just want to name how uncomfortable that assembly made me feel." His concern resonated with several other staff members and the room became abuzz with chatter. The student government had had the event's agenda approved by a white staff member, and it was clear that she had not registered the problem of having a watermelon eating contest at a school in the Bronx with a significant African-American student population, and a disproportionately white staff. The principal, needing to continue the staff meeting, asked those concerned to stay after to discuss the situation with the proper time and attention that it deserved.

A group of us gathered around a large table and formed a plan to address what had happened. It was reassuring that the principal was at this circle discussion, showing that all levels of leadership were invested in a restorative response. A few of the teachers suggested that we make the event a teachable moment, and that we create and deliver a mini-lesson for students that would illuminate the issue. As I was already working on some lessons surrounding the civil rights era and cultural competency in my classes, I volunteered to take the lead on creating content.

The following Monday, we taught this lesson on racial iconography in America as a tool of oppression in our classes school-wide. This would ensure that all students were at least aware of the history and impact of racialized imagery that might have been triggered by our watermelon eating contest. We also agreed that we would hold a circle discussion with members of the student government and interested staff members. As I had experience in this type of discussion format, I agreed to facilitate the circle.

On Monday we gathered the students and staff into a circle of about 20 people. We already knew through some pre-circle discussion that the harm of the event had not been intended by the students or the staff who had overseen the planning, and so we started with the staff members sharing how they were affected. One powerful share came from an African-American teacher who had grown up in Birmingham, Alabama. Her description of the racism she had experienced first hand was powerful and grabbed the attention of the students, even those who had previously vocalized that they didn't understand "why we're making such a big deal out of this." Soon it was clear to all that the assembly had, indeed, affected our community, even if it was unintentional. Genuine apologies were volunteered by the students, and as teachers we all agreed that we needed to work harder to help students connect what we were teaching in our classes with their own actions and choices in real-world settings. The tough part in all of this was that we knew the students had not intended to make fun of black folks, and that there was no malice behind the event. But we also knew that, as a community, we needed to make this a teachable moment. After the talking piece had been passed around for the final time, we thanked everyone for being vulnerable enough to participate, and I think we all felt better having shared and heard from one another.

Lauren, New York

Story debrief

I see this event and the restorative response as a catalyst and turning point for our school. For several years, even before I arrived, we had had a variety of restorative practices and a peer mediation program in place, but they were not always employed or supported to the fullest extent. One thing that this event did for the school was to cement our need for these types of processes when addressing tough issues. It served to bring us closer as a staff and to speed up our move, as a community, towards this enhanced approach of addressing conflict. The careful and restorative response that we gave to this event felt good to the folks involved. The principal went on to create a full-time RJ coordinator position the next year, a role I was asked to fill. Following this incident, we began to have brief "culture and counseling" check-ins on a daily basis. This helps us, for example, to ensure that re-entry meetings are happening after a student is removed from class, and that all the support services are connected and communicating effectively. The overseeing of these meetings between deans and counselors is now a part of my role. In fact, there were a lot of things that we systematized in the following year due to this event, giving importance to such topics as cultural relevancy and ensuring that it is included in our classes and professional development (PD).

I think the potential of this work is to disrupt violence of all kinds as we see it in our communities. It's empowering to people to say, "This is our community," and if we don't like what we are seeing, we have the power to gather ourselves and make changes. Sometimes students will say, "I'm just one person, what can I do?" Our school is now showing people that they do have power and influence in their community, and that they can have a real impact.

7

Resistant Staff

WAYS TO UNDERSTAND AND WORK
THROUGH PUSH-BACK

Understanding and working through staff skepticism of a restorative mindset shift

We can learn to love resistant staff... Okay, so you must be thinking, *come on, nobody loves resistant staff!* And it's true that when you are trying to make the shift to a restorative mindset, having even a few teachers, support personnel, or administrators giving push-back can be downright exhausting. Certainly, our significant others have sat patiently through several dinner time venting sessions listening to our frustrations on this topic. But just as we ask students to see their biggest challenges and mistakes as opportunities for reflection and personal growth, we invite you to see working with resistant staff as an opportunity for sharpening your own practice and delivering meaningful change more effectively. After all, shifting mindsets of those folks who might not yet be on board is where the true work lives. This applies to skeptical students and parents as well. So, while it might not be as fun as collaborating with like-minded co-workers, let's take a look at ways to understand and embrace resistant staff with mindfulness and heart. It is not about winning an argument about RJ, or forcing through your agenda; it must be about listening to and learning from one another.

There are a variety of reasons that might make staff resistant to changing their perspective on school discipline and culture, but the one that you will never likely encounter is, "Our current discipline system is working perfectly and we don't want to change it!" Almost universally, educators feel the same need to address discipline as everyone else at the school, but some folks just feel that there needs to be even more harsh consequences given out to control student behavior, a "get tough on crime mentality." It's important to remember that we all share the same goal of positive student behavior, overall academic success, and personal growth in school. Despite the fact that traditional discipline has been shown to be ineffective at achieving these goals and by other metrics, RJ-resistant staff often see detention and suspension as the only *real* form of discipline, the only way to show misbehaving students that you are serious about behavior expectations. Another way to say it is that the most common push-back you will come across is a fear that "nothing will happen" in a restorative system, the concern that students will "walk all over you" or "get away with anything." This might also occur as statements such as, "I don't think sitting around in a circle holding hands is going to solve anything" or "All a student has to do is say sorry or write a poem and they get off scot free!" These are very common misconceptions and apprehensions about the use of RJ. Does any of this sound familiar? Even though these statements are contrary to how RJ actually works, some staff may have this perception based on something they have heard or if they have already had a negative experience with a restorative shift at their past or current school—that RJ is nothing more than a chance for students to fake remorse and avoid consequence is a misconception that would make anyone skeptical of this work. It is important to understand where this fear and push-back are coming from (sometimes you can even ask!), and to really understand how the staff came to these beliefs.

Skepticism based on these common fears can often be grouped into three categories, as illustrated wonderfully by Daniel Levine (who happens to be David's brother!), formerly of the Baltimore Community Mediation Center (BCMC):

Push-back may stem from one or more genuine needs of staff members:

a. I want to be confident this won't happen again (deterrence).

b. I want them to understand what they did was wrong (expression).

c. I want them to feel as bad as I felt (fairness).

When looked at it this way, the fear or concern makes perfect sense. People want to make sure that their needs are met, and they are apprehensive that the restorative approach may not satisfy these needs. Items 'a' and 'b' are pretty universal desires of educators. Item 'c' is rarely expressed outright, but might be lurking below the surface when someone is feeling harmed.

Staff resistant to RJ may think that suspensions address all of these items, but we strongly believe that traditional (exclusionary) forms of discipline often fail to satisfy the needs of those involved, and that restorative practices are far more effective at addressing and repairing harm and addressing the needs of those involved. The point of this chapter is about working with resistant staff, not making a case for RJ, but let's take a look at each need for a moment.

a) I want to be confident this won't happen again (deterrence)

Detentions and suspensions have been shown to be quite *ineffective* at preventing recidivism. Often a student suspended will feel angry and grow more defiant after a suspension. They may feel angry if they were unfairly punished, or if they felt unheard, or if someone else involved did not receive a punishment. Without voice and a conversation, kids will often blame adults for their actions and the "trouble" they got into. So, feeling pushed away from the community, angry, and without closure to the original incident, it is no wonder these retributive discipline measures don't help the student to understand and improve their behavior. Make students feel like they don't belong, and they might just act out to get attention from the community by force. Not to mention that even one suspension has been linked to doubling a student's chance of dropping out of school. That is reason enough to be very careful with how and when we use suspensions in our schools.

On the other hand, a student who has engaged in a restorative circle where all voices are valued, including their own, where the incident is carefully discussed, will have a chance to feel heard, to learn empathy by hearing from those impacted, and will be able to participate in repairing the harm, improving their sense of agency. Making sure that there are no unresolved issues around the incident and positively working to keep the student within the community can work magic at preventing further incidents of harm.

b) I want them to understand what they did was wrong (expression)

Suspensions and detentions will make clear the fact that a rule was broken and that they are being punished, but this most often will not get at the root of the issue for a student. Take, for example, a student who is being teased every day who finally punches their bully. They may get suspended for the punch, but they may feel justified in their actions. In this way, a suspension will not convince them of wrongdoing or give them any skills to handle a similar situation in the future any differently. It may also spark more incidents of aggression with the student and their bully.

Conversely, in a restorative circle or peer mediation with these students, the teasing student may get to hear how much impact their words have and take responsibility. The student who threw the punch may hear and consider other ways that the situation could be handled, and both students can be empowered to take actions to repair the harm to each other and their school in a way that is based on accountability and not shame.

c) I want them to feel as bad as I felt (fairness)

Does it feel bad to be suspended? Well, a lot depends on the situation at home. Students may get grounded by a parent, even beaten by a parent, or nothing may happen. The results vary wildly. Often there is no adult at home during a suspension and the student is left unsupervised, which can lead to greater problems. It is true that a suspension may introduce shame or punishment by family, but it is very hard to tell what effect it may have in a traditional system because the student is often not debriefed in any way. The message is sent that "You do not belong here at school" for a while, and then they simply return without much debrief.

Advocates of traditional discipline will argue that suspensions send a clear message that the behavior was unacceptable. We can all agree that this is a message we would like to send after a harmful act. However, this message is not necessarily even stated clearly to a student when they are suspended. The same message is not only *implied* in a restorative setting; impacted community members get to say it with words to the student's face, looking them in the eye and carefully explaining how they were harmed and what needs to happen to make it right. This can be far more healing for a victim than simply seeing them get suspended. Getting to express as a teacher how upset the student had made you and to hear their reaction can lead to much greater closure than kicking them out of class and awaiting their awkward and often tense return to class.

This RJ work is deeply personal work. Usually there is a small cadre of teachers leading the RJ push, or perhaps a principal or superintendent who gets it immediately. They understand that we are not going to be able to punish our way into positive behavior. And that we also cannot sit by and be permissive when students or adults are harming the community. So these are the people who want a healthy and safe learning environment for all, but who have seen the disproportionality of discipline in the past and also understand that increasing punitive punishments is not leading to the desired outcomes. To these folks, when they encounter RJ, it makes a lot of sense. Our belief has always been that it is extremely wise to continue working with that group of folks, especially in the face of resistance. Invest time and energy, working with this motivated group, supporting them and allowing them to thrive. They will be the ones to provide strong examples of this working in their classrooms, and this, more than any philosophical argument or mandated professional development, will begin to win over other members of the staff community. Show, don't tell, works particularly well when rolling out RJ initiatives.

This is not rocket science—building strong and authentic relationships with students to achieve desired outcomes seems pretty logical; trying to punish students and exclude them seems rather insane.

Nicholas recalls his mother doing this work in the 1980s, without it being known as RJ. His mother was teaching a 4th grade class and there was a student who was bigger and louder than the other students and who was known to be problematic to most of the staff. Nicholas' mother simply took the time to get to know him, talked with him kindly, and gave him some of the extra attention he needed. Over time, he became her "right-hand man," doing extra chores around the classroom and getting his work done. He felt like he was wanted in the class, rather than a problem; he felt heard and seen and cared for by his teacher, and that gave him the confidence to try his best. Other teachers were shocked at the positive results. Many reading this book may know or may themselves already be this type of teacher. Even some RJ-resistant staff members may be this type of teacher, not realizing that building strong relationships and working to repair them when harmed is the bread and butter of RJ. To most teachers like this, RJ simply provides a label for much of the work they have already been doing, and provides systems to support their work in the classroom.

Similar to Nicholas, David's mother provided a strong example of RJ principles when she was unaware of this term but was doing the work none the less. While working as an Employment Counselor in New York State prisons, she helped inmates draft their resumes, make life goals, and prepare for job searching once they left prison. Rather than judging them for their past mistakes, or focusing on the vast differences in their cultures (his mom was an older white lady from rural Massachusetts, while most of the inmates were young men of color from NYC), she approached them with obvious love and compassion. She got to know them personally and shared details about her own life and choices. She also "kept it real," calling them out when she felt they were making excuses or not working to their potential. And most of all, she had high expectations that made them want to work hard. They could tell how much she believed that they could be successful when they left prison, and she gave them tools and tips on how to navigate the world. For this, like Nicholas' mother, she was repaid with a great deal of positive results, good attendance at her classes, gifts of artwork and other tokens of appreciation, and respect. Suddenly some of the toughest inmates would get incredibly mad if anyone so much as looked at his mother sideways. This, at the core, is all that RJ is—treating the people you are working with as equals, as humans, and as valued members of the community who have the power to do great things, maintaining high expectations through support and honest conversation rather than punishment and threats. Once resistant staff realize that this is what RJ is all about, they are often not so resistant.

A positive take on push-back

Okay, so we have looked at some of the reasons why staff can be resistant to RJ philosophy and policies, and how RJ can effectively address those worries. Now let's look at ways that this push-back can actually improve your skills as a facilitator. After all, this is why you can love resistant staff—they might help you sharpen your message and become a better advocate for students.

- *Clarity of message:* You will need to have a crystal-clear understanding of what you are trying to accomplish, and you will need to prepare more thoroughly, knowing that there are some dissenting voices amongst those you are trying to reach. Nothing will help you clarify your intentions and your mission more than having to persuade others of your new system's efficacy. From preparing your explanation of what RJ is, to preparing staff PD materials, knowing that you might have opposition will really push you to refine your approach, back your arguments up with research, and remain open-minded to other opinions, creating a democratic space where all voices can be heard.

- *Practicing what you preach:* This can be a chance to "put your money where your mouth is." Are you really invested in having tough conversations and forging relationships with those in your community who differ from you? Then you really need to make sure you are using restorative practices in meetings, PD, and to address staff harm when it occurs. After all, this is what we are asking of students. What you will quickly see is that it can be quite uncomfortable to communicate, to be vulnerable, and to try and find common ground with other staff you may not agree with or with whom you may have had negative interactions in the past. But what an enlightening experience, to actually *feel* what it must be like for students to engage in this work with each other, building community with other students they don't know, or sitting in a circle to discuss an incident of harm. It's *very* challenging, and not many of us have been in the same position that we ask students to be. Try sitting down to talk with a person at your school you don't get along with and you will quickly see why a lot of students would actually prefer a suspension rather than having to talk with the person with whom they had a conflict. And yet, having this experience yourself will build your empathy immensely for anyone engaging in this work. It will also model the exact type of behavior you are proposing, building community, having tough conversations, being authentic and brave, taking ownership of your agency.

- *Staff community:* Anyone promoting restorative practices across a school will only benefit from bringing the same work to staff and staff meetings. As mentioned above, why would we do anything with students that we don't find useful ourselves? And by engaging in these activities as a staff member you will see the community and relationships grow immensely. When there are skeptical members of staff, this should drive an extra effort to build staff community and bonding through fun activities. What starts as a difference of opinion can actually bring a group closer together in the end, if there is a restorative space in which to communicate.

- *Increased perspective:* We believe that diversity at every level is a positive thing. If everyone had the same ideas as you, then you may actually have a narrow view of what is possible in your community. Staff are resistant not just because they fear change, but because they are coming from a different background or belief system. Their ideas need to be heard and considered, and they may actually speak to the needs or concerns of some students or families. Staying open to others' ideas and opinions can possibly add something new to your practice and improve your system, especially if this is a community that you came to as an outsider— authentically seeking to understand local culture, attitudes, norms, etc. is the only way to show that you are true to your intention of inclusion, equity, and justice. Try to get to the core of what those staff believe and want, look for common ground and what approaches they have employed successfully that may benefit the RJ system you are building. Listen, and you just may learn something.

Ways to engage and embrace resistant staff
If you really care, then ask!
The fear that "nothing happens" (that is, no consequences) to a student in a restorative system who has caused harm or broken community values can arise from several avenues. Commonly people might have had (or heard) a negative experience with RJ, or

even more common, heard a falsehood about RJ like, "He punched a kid, then he drew a picture about it and nothing happened to him!" Most often it doesn't happen this way, although you never know someone's previous experience with restorative practices (until you ask!). So it's a great idea to have a conversation with staff and students about what their experience or knowledge of restorative practice has been previously. It is also best to include people when building the restorative system you plan to implement. Having a variety of voices will only help with buy-in, participation, and strengthening your goals.

Don't isolate—communicate!

When RJ is used to address a specific incident that has occurred, make sure that as many affected people as possible are present at any resulting mediations or circles, and find an appropriate way to communicate to staff *all* the work that goes into a restorative action. Depending on what level of confidentiality you are dealing with, make sure that you have communicated as much as you can. At one school where we worked, we had a weekly RJ newsletter that addressed actions. For instance, in the case mentioned above, rather than hearing a rumor about what happened in the RJ office after a fight, we might have sent out a note on the incident to all staff:

> As many of you may have heard, we unfortunately had a physical fight in the hallway on Friday. We had a successful peer mediation after school on Tuesday and the two students seem to be friends again. A restorative contract circle was held for the student who was the physical aggressor (the author of the act), after school on Wednesday with the author, the author's mother and aunt, the counselor, and vice principal. After a lengthy discussion, accountability was taken and we worked to repair the harm. He agreed that four after-school counseling sessions would be more useful than detention, and being that writing was a strength, he would write four poems about anger and read them at freshman

classes next week. We all felt that this would be a great way to model self-reflection and growth for those younger students and give back to the community he had harmed. Because his mother had to leave work to come to pick him up he also offered to cook two dinners to help out at home and give back—he would rather be seen by others as a great cook than a great fighter, for reasons that we discussed. Everyone there agreed that these would be meaningful and powerful consequences for his actions. If he meets all of these items by the allotted dates, as well as avoiding any near-term confrontations, he will fulfill his contract and be allowed to stay part of our school community without suspension. Please let us know if you observe any relevant behavior (positive or negative in the next two weeks), or if you have any concerns or questions about these logical consequences for his actions.

This may not assuage all detractors, but it shows the scope of the work, humanizes the student, and allows anyone to comment on the restorative plan. By the nature of the process, any affected staff present at the circle should be satisfied with the contract created. Everyone should be asked if they feel that the proposed consequences are meaningful and sufficient, so that they are free to voice any concerns before the conference is concluded. Usually after even just one circle, staff understand more and are on board with the approach. An important point is to make sure to follow up if the student does not meet the goals and that consequences are triggered as promised (a new circle, a new intervention, or even sometimes a traditional detention or suspension), so that the contracts seem valid and legitimate.

Bring them into the fold!

It's easy to be skeptical of the *idea* of instituting restorative practices, but in our experience, once folks have experienced these practices in real life, most walk away convinced of their power and effectiveness. So it's important to directly involve as many teachers, administrators, families, and students in the restorative practices that you are trying to promote. Of course this includes having their voices present at relevant restorative conferences after an incident has occurred, but also having them as a part of community-building and discussion circles or any other activity that fosters deeper relationships and connection as you build your system. This will quickly de-mystify the process and show how fun and powerful these activities can be.

At one school where David has worked, there was an RJ office where he, another dean, a vice principal, and a few students engaged in the bulk of the restorative actions after any harm occurred. When the school got a new principal, he had a brilliant idea. Many teachers' schedules had one or two paid class periods where they were not teaching. These periods could be utilized by administration in any way that would benefit planning, administration, school success, etc. The new principal proposed using some of these periods to have teachers spend time in the RJ office, to help out and observe what they did on a daily basis. Intentionally, he assigned excited teachers who had volunteered as well as some staff who remained skeptical or uninformed of restorative practices. This was a bit scary for everyone, but then, in reality, it was enlightening. The staff saw that mostly what occurred was talking with upset students in the same way that they, as teachers, often did at the end of a class. Many of them were already acting quite restoratively in their classrooms, and their time in the RJ office felt natural. The RJ team would ask the visiting teachers, "What do you think we should do?" in response to an incident or troubled student, and usually their ideas were as restorative as anyone's! They might suggest talking with a coach the student respected or calling a family member to discuss, but most often it was just to try to sit down with them in an authentic way and to find out what was really going on and how they could help get them back on track. They never realized just how restorative they already were acting, and how what we were doing behind the closed door of the RJ office was a lot like what they were already doing as passionate educators. When they joined in on circles in the RJ office they often suggested very constructive and meaningful consequences other than suspension or silent detention, and found that they often had a lot to offer the students as support. In one such circle, a teacher offered that instead of detention they could come to four of her after-school math tutoring sessions to help younger students. This teacher had previously taught the student in the circle and knew how good they were at math. She saw that having the student come assist would be a consequence as well as a much needed help to her struggling students as the state exam approached. In all instances, even folks who claimed to be "not into this RJ thing" were always into sitting down with students to talk and see what was going on and try to help. Turns out most of them actually were "into this RJ thing!" A lot of times teachers have trouble engaging in RJ after they have been personally harmed by a student, and seeing the process from the outside, when they have not been directly affected by an action, helped make the benefits more easily apparent, and the process more accessible.

If you preach it, teach it!

If you are going to ask educators to use restorative practices with students, it should also be used with staff. After all, why would we ask students to engage in something that we, as adults, don't see value in ourselves? A great place to start is dedicating some time during staff meetings to model and practice RJ activities, such as community-building circles and activities, role-playing, de-escalation, and open discussions.

In the same way that we ask students to use instructional time to do these activities, we, too, must see the value in making space for them in our own busy schedules as educators and administrators. A staff that is bonded closely will be much more supportive and effective as a whole. In some staff training we have asked the group to "pair and share" to this question:

What types of discipline did you experience when you were in school, and how effective were they?

We love asking this question because it shows just how many teachers struggled with discipline and behavior in their youth, how many times they faced detention or suspension, and how few times that approach actually worked to help guide them through conflict. As you could guess, they all made it through troubled times eventually and went on to college and a career, allowing them the credentials to hold their current job. So, we ask, "If traditional discipline wasn't that effective, what helped you turn your life around and become so successful to be here today?" Usually the answer is that they were grateful for support they got from a teacher, or family member, a positive experience such as a college trip or winning an award, or strong relationships such as on a sports team. With that history in mind, we could then open the discussion wider and consider new ways to address discipline most effectively at the school.

Bringing resistant or skeptical staff into the RJ fold

It's important to have skeptical staff sit in on well-facilitated circles, restorative conferences, and role-playing practices. Try to have a small cadre of interested kids trained and facilitating circles around the school. Say, "Hey, on Monday, you all are going to be going out in pairs (with an adult support) and running circles in classrooms across the school." This changes the game by involving many in the community to help develop the systems themselves, rather than it being a top-down initiative coming from the administration.

We always recommend training a small group of folks (adults and youth) who do this work really well, reflect on it, keep pushing out into the school, reflect again, and keep building. Start with a small invested group within the community, and continue to support them and help them build outwards.

Other worries
Toxic mindsets
Sometimes you may deal not just with resistant staff, but also toxic and harmful staff, those who are actively working against equity, openly with bias, and opposed to being in a relationship with

students. This is extremely rare, but unfortunately it does happen. Sure, we could advocate that administrators fire or remove these teachers, but that is not really the point; we want community change, not just a school change. So we don't want to shift those folks to another school; we need to create a space where we can have those tough conversations, where we can say, "Hey, what you are doing is impacting students and I see it. We see it." Sometimes that is enough. But we need to create these spaces where change can occur. Ideally, yes, this would systematically change over time. We would love to see restorative systems written into contracts at a union level. Occasionally we have sat in on conferences where an adult has harmed a student and there is no precedent or contract requirement that they engage in a circle or address this harm. Teachers may claim in cases that they do not have to speak with a student human to human, and they will not. They may feel they are above the student and should be respected as the authority, regardless of their own behavior. There is usually a fear or traumatic experience at the base of this attitude, and it may be difficult to engage this person, especially if they are constantly trying to weaponize the union contract against your efforts. We need to build a positive culture around them, and look for ways to include them. This is really where you need to walk the walk of "we are better as a community with everyone included."

It won't always be easy to shift mindsets towards a restorative approach, but if we want to make it happen, we must be willing to be open and transparent, communicate clearly, remain inclusive, and see all the ways that a diversity of opinions can help us grow and learn from each other.

FROM SKEPTIC TO ADVOCATE

Walking back into my middle school classroom after being out the previous day at a training, I first noticed that the colorful plastic chairs were not stacked neatly on desks as they usually are. I could also see some paper scattered on the floor; usually my students are great about following the clean-up routine.

It all made sense when I saw the note on my desk, handwritten from the substitute, and it was not good. I almost couldn't believe the long list of negative comments and anecdotes she had left about what I always considered a well-behaved group of students. I guess the real test is how students behave when their regular teacher is away.

I made sure to find one or two students from the class, the ones I knew to be upfront and honest, and I asked them what exactly had happened. It turns out the note was pretty accurate: most of them were not listening to the sub, were getting out of their chairs and making a mess, and, most concerning, they had begun to make fun of the sub for speaking with a heavy accent. I was deeply saddened and knew that this needed to be addressed.

This was my first year teaching in the Pacific Northwest, and I knew that they did some things, including discipline, a bit different from where I had previously taught in Florida. I was first introduced to the idea of RJ at some of our staff meetings.

I was unfamiliar with it and, to be frank, skeptical. The idea of it, at first, seemed like an excuse for students to get out of any consequences for their actions. And the concept of sitting around in a circle and sharing personal details seemed a bit awkward and cheesy.

But honestly, I started to really enjoy these circles; I was laughing with my co-workers, learning about them, and forming bonds more quickly than I had in years at my previous school. So, after this incident with my students misbehaving, I decided to give it a try in my classroom. I invited Gabriella, the staff member who offered facilitation, to come in and address the incident.

Tears and empathy

I wasn't sure what to expect as I sat in the same plastic chair as my students and as Gabriella took over. She explained how the circle would work and started asking questions that we all took turns responding to. I remember that one of the questions was about a time when we had personally experienced bullying. Within minutes, my students started sharing some emotional and heartfelt experiences where they had felt hurt by bullying or seen it happen.

I was amazed at how maturely the whole group was listening and how genuinely they were sharing. It was almost like they were just waiting for a chance to get these things off their chest. I shared a story from my childhood and I could see students sitting on the edge of their seat to hear.

At one point, after someone had shared a particularly heart-breaking story, almost everyone in the group was in tears. Gabriella then connected these stories to what had happened when the substitute was in our class. She asked the group to share how they think she must have felt when she was being teased for her accent, something over which she had no control.

I could almost see some of the students making empathetic connections in their young minds. Quickly they expressed how miserable that must have felt for the woman. Many of them even related it to their own stories of bullying.

I was impressed by this, but the true test of this work came the following week when again I needed to be out of the building and the same substitute returned. You can imagine my anxiousness to read the note from the sub and my elation to hear that things had gone incredibly well this time around!

I was already warming up to restorative practices, but this experience really cemented my commitment of forging deeper relationships with my students. I have the same pressure at this school as at my last one to cover content and prepare students for state exams, but I actually think investing the time in circles like this helps us to work faster as a group, and with more trust and communication overall.

I think about what would have happened back in Florida. Probably some of the more disrespectful students would have been singled out for detention. They would have sat in silence after school for the same amount of time that we sat as a classroom circle with Gabriella. But the whole group would have missed out on this valuable experience and a rare chance to develop empathy. Probably the students who would have received detention would feel embarrassed or upset thinking about what had happened to them, rather than reflecting deeply on how their actions had affected others.

I think it's easy to be resistant to the idea of RJ, but once you have been involved in it in real life, it's hard not to become excited about its vast potential to improve our classrooms, even when we aren't around.

Kelsey, Washington

Story debrief

As you can see, being authentically exposed to and involved in restorative practices is what was able to open Kelsey's eyes to the power and efficacy of RJ as a tool. Had she simply been told by the administration that she must start using these practices, she may have remained guarded and resistant. But she was provided with adequate staff training, and a useful tool that felt like a help rather than a burden. This led to her willing involvement and ultimately her enthusiasm for the process.

PART II

NEVER FORGET WHERE YOU CAME FROM

8

Roots

BRIEF HISTORY OF RESTORATIVE JUSTICE

As we frame this book as a guide and theoretical basis for RJ, we can't proceed without a clear statement of gratitude for those who have paved the way, those who began the modern movement in the early and mid-1980s, those who fought against entrenched forces in the justice and educational systems. We thank you for the work and passion you brought to your communities and our communities around the world. As this movement grows and as we continue to change systems we need stronger theory and practices that move RJ beyond victim offender conferences.

Nicholas speaks...

As the founder of the NC4RJ, both my own roots and the roots of RJ are important to understand. While I can speak with great authority on my own roots, it is hard to cover the breadth of RJ in a single chapter. There isn't a definitive book that captures the history and influence of RJ, but a few books in our community speak more in detail about its origins. These are a collection of essays that help provide the diversity of perspectives and histories of RJ: *Handbook of Restorative Justice: A Global Perspective*,[1] *A*

---

1   Sullivan, D. (2007) *Handbook of Restorative Justice: A Global Perspective.* Abingdon: Routledge.

Restorative Justice Reader,[2] and, most recently and importantly, *Colorizing Restorative Justice: Voicing Our Realities.*[3]

We'd like to share a brief history of RJ: RJ is a modern term and there is currently great debate about what it means and how to use the term properly. That said, if I can speak with some overarching generalities, I will take that step. The modern RJ movement is an outgrowth of the collision of Aboriginal, First Nations, Native American, African and Polynesian tribal practices (indigenous peoples), and the Western justice/governmental systems. During the late 1970s and early 1980s a few governments took steps to learn from indigenous practices to improve their own systems. Two stand out in particular: the Truth and Reconciliation Commission after the end of the apartheid in South Africa, and "family group conferencing" at the intersection of Māori tribal governments and New Zealand's government. These two examples of RJ are held as the beginning of a modern movement. They are certainly not the only starting points, but give some context for our global community.

My first exposure was to the Māori traditions. When I learned about their history I learned about both family group conferencing (family harm/issues) and restorative conferences (crime). The Māori people, like many colonized people, had experienced significant violence and trauma perpetrated by white colonizers resulting in the destruction (damage) of their economic, familial, and cultural systems. During the 1970s, similar to the American Indian Movement (AIM) in the USA, they were experiencing heightened organization and agency. Ultimately, they wanted to take back power and decision-making and create their own systems that would support a cultural resurgence and at the same time deal with the violence and family difficulties their community was experiencing. In this way family group conferencing was "born." This process of supporting family units to deal with their difficulties with the support of extended family units and the tribe became a

2   Johnstone, G. (ed.) (2012) *A Restorative Justice Reader* (Second edn). Abingdon: Routledge.
3   Valandra, E.C. (ed.) (2020) *Colorizing Restorative Justice: Voicing Our Realities.* St Paul, MN: Living Justice Press.

huge success in repairing culture, enabling families to heal, creating trust, rebuilding economic systems, and even repairing some of the harm done by the New Zealand government.

I believe that as an outgrowth of the success of RJ and power sharing, the New Zealand government has agreed to pay reparations to some tribes, they are currently in dialogue with other tribes, they are making land concessions, and they are making public apologies to the Māori tribes. I believe that power sharing and accountability to the harm caused are fundamental to a restorative mindset. (Our principles of agency and engaging all stakeholders stand out in these examples—the government is publicly taking responsibility for their actions.)

While you see a very clear picture of RJ in the story and experience of the Māori people, the legacy of apartheid and the resulting Truth and Reconciliation Commission in South Africa attempted to heal a nation after generations of exploitation and oppression. To reiterate a primary point, these examples of RJ are both just examples, and early examples as well. This means that there hadn't been the decades of iterations on the learning that started in South Africa and New Zealand that we have now. These were brave attempts at healing from generational violence and trauma. RJ is on a continuum that works towards a "more just system" and responses to harm and violence (systemic or acute). At the end of the apartheid system of segregation and state-sanctioned violence against Black Africans, the state tried to create a mechanism for repairing and talking about the violence and atrocities that had occurred. No one is claiming this system or structure was perfect, but given the extreme nature of the healing that was needed, they had to create a national project for repair. The main thrust of the Truth and Reconciliation Commission was to create space for authors of violence or other crimes to take responsibility for those actions and for victims to ask for reparations. If authors took responsibility for their crimes and they were politically motivated, there was an opportunity for amnesty. A small proportion of applications were actually granted amnesty. Besides the nature of these hearings, an incredibly important aspect was their public nature. While many families around South Africa didn't have television, many, if not most, had access to a radio. Nearly all the hearings were broadcast, with high-profile cases broadcast on the weekend for everyone to hear. This type of public accountability was essential for the newly formed democratic government to be successful.

Had South Africa not had the public accounting of its past violence there would be no way to move forward. There is a saying in AA (Alcoholics Anonymous), "You're only as sick as your secrets." We often refuse to make space for even the voicing of the actions; this makes our communities sicker.

I want to reiterate that these are just two examples of early RJ systems and experiences. Other areas that maintained or restarted traditions were the Massai people, First Nations people in many locations in North America, and indigenous people in the South Pacific. There are also other traditions that we may not know of yet... It is our belief that RJ is a human practice and can be seen in a variety of forms throughout the world. Due to the nature of British colonization, these experiences in RJ quickly moved throughout the formerly British colonized world (the Commonwealth).

It is also important to note many sects of Western religions have also supported RJ. In America the Mennonites can take center stage—Howard Zehr is one of the foremost RJ academics as a professor at the Eastern Mennonite University.

While I say the modern RJ movements have their roots in indigenous cultures, it is also my belief that this is deeply human work, as you see examples of RJ-type systems around the world in Western culture and indigenous cultures and everywhere in between. Many world religions also have RJ tendencies and have had a great influence on this movement.

Nicholas' personal roots in restorative justice, and what has influenced his evolution...

As I've mentioned, I am an educator by passion and training. I certainly fall on the "progressive education" side of the debate.

Young people should be given agency in their learning. They can pursue their interests, and with guidance we can create systems that encourage a breadth of knowledge. I come from a family of educators and was excited about becoming a teacher. As a certified teacher in Vermont I took an opportunity to volunteer at the local community justice center (CJC)—in Vermont each county is served by a CJC. In the evening I was a panel member for youth who were in trouble with the law.

Early in my own RJ learning I was exposed to two influential leaders in our community, the first being Jon Kidde, the first director of Restorative Justice for Oakland Youth (RJOY)—this organization is a national leader for RJ. Jon comes from a public health background and has an amazing perspective on this work. Fania Davis, the sister of the acclaimed civil rights activist Angela Davis and a civil rights activist in her own right, was instrumental in founding this organization.

I was incredibly lucky to meet and work with Jon during a time in my life where I had the space and excitement to soak up all the knowledge. He and I shared a number of hours learning and talking about RJ. I invited him to lead some training sessions at organizations I worked for. During this time I worked in the evening at a local "half-way house" for young men returning from prison.

My work in the "half-way house" was instrumental in how I came to better understand justice. Many of us have done bad or hurtful things, especially when we were young. Fortunately, we're not defined by those deeds. For those who maybe did something more serious, made a bigger mistake, or in some cases just happened to get caught, they are defined by their actions, and we label them "criminals" and "felons." I started meeting and working with those young men with caution and concern in my mind. I was "worried." I walked into a room with six to nine young men not much younger than I was, and bigger in many cases. Yes, I was on guard. It took weeks for me to realize that they are, in all ways except one, just like me. They wanted to be free, to work, and to be with family (their own wives and children, their parents, and friends). I was lucky to meet these men who'd been tangled up with the justice system at a young age, seeing the impact it had had on their lives. At the same time I was learning about RJ. I was able to challenge myself to first seek relationships with the residents, and to see them as humans first and foremost.

All too often we see a scary kid or hear stories from their middle school or 4th grade teacher, and we come into that relationship on guard...especially if the student is black or brown and you're a white person. As it took me weeks to realize that these young men weren't that different from myself, it might take you time to get comfortable with the young people in your class or school. The important thing to remember is that this is *your* work, not the responsibility of youth.

Some time later, in 2014 and 2016, I had the opportunity to meet and talk with Fania Davis and other members of the RJOY team, including the director of the Oakland Unified School District (OUSD) RJ program David Yusom. These people and the Oakland community are an inspiration to me and will hopefully continue to inspire our communities around the country to do better when it comes to conflict both inside and outside the school building. What I continue to take away from these opportunities to learn is that RJ is much more than a way of dealing with transgression; it is a way of *being in the world*. If I can be more relationship-focused and find opportunities to connect and then understand the harm or conflict, I will be better able to maintain those relationships and to be in a meaningful community.

During that same early time (2010) I was lucky enough to see and attend training by Dominic Barter in Vermont. Dominic is an amazing RJ international leader. He is British, but lives and works in Brazil. His work is deeply connected to systemic issues of poverty and community, and he has worked tirelessly to improve a disastrous juvenile justice system and support schools in reforming their discipline systems. At the time, in addition to running an after-school program, I was working with young adults who were returning to the community after time in state prison. Not only did the training with Dominic speak to my personal mission; it directly connected to the work I was doing at the "half-way house." I found direct connections between his work in humanizing the justice system and humanizing our experience of daily life. It really is, "How can I be a better human?" both to myself and to others.

During the training one thing stood out to me, and I want you to ask yourself this same question. We did an exercise where we partnered up and shared, "What is a conflict you are currently having?" Now, not everyone had the opportunity to share, but four or five people were able to share a story of a conflict. At that moment I was connecting to these stories. Later...I realized that everyone took the victim's perspective. As I mentioned prior, I was working with youth. I had experienced young people doing the same thing, focusing on the harm done by others to themselves. That experience of people sharing their victimhood should remind us that we rarely need help being the victim (impacted person)... What we need help with is our experience of being the oppressor or the author of the harm (see Chapter 5 for more on how this relates to racial justice).

As you think about times that you were in conflict, I am sure a number of examples pop into your head. Some examples may jump to mind—a work colleague who can't seem to reply to an email, a student who never listens, a loved partner who can't seem to put their dishes in the sink until the next day. Now I want you to think about a time when you might have been short, condescending, dismissive, or sarcastic to that colleague, student, or partner. This is what I mean when I ask you to think not only about being a victim in conflict, but also a contributor to conflict.

As a teacher I have to constantly reflect on how the student would experience me or my communication. When you think about conflict and harm, challenge yourself to see the harm you cause others. It is often the hardest thing to see. From these experiences and countless other hours of study, reflection, and deliberation with others we come to the framework of RJ that helps us both communicate the ideas and implement some changes that will help equip schools and educators with the tools to effectively engage with justice. I am grateful that these early trainings helped me to re-evaluate my perspective on conflict and harm, and this book is designed to help you illuminate the aspects that might not be immediately apparent.

Restorative justice
A way of being

While we speak primarily to an education setting, you can do this at home, at work, or in your community. We define RJ as a "relational approach to conflict," which often seems insufficient to capture the scope of the work. RJ is a relational approach to relationships, schools, basketball teams, families, parenting, love, disagreements, hope, and so much more...*it is a relational approach to everything*. This is why this work is immensely personal to us at the NC4RJ, and to many of the people with whom we work. Our hope is that this book will be both informative to the theory and also provide you with stories from practitioners that capture these ideas.

When we think about implementing RJ in a school we do a lot of thinking first about how this is a personal journey. If you are engaging with RJ because you think it is a great way to "fix kids" or it is some kind of program to implement, then this isn't the book for you. Like all equity work, this is not a technical solution—*this is a way of being*. When we think about where to begin implementation of RJ, we always start with staff culture. When we structure our first ideas, workshops, and trainings as "adult first" work, we implant the seed of "this is work we do as educators, not a practice that we administer to kids." Somehow we often forget that teachers are people too. It is almost shocking how emotive staff will be when they are given just a modicum of space to share their hopes, dreams, fears, and concerns. I have had new teachers speak about the challenges and tribulations of learning how to be good teachers, and I have had veteran teachers speak about the concern they have for students in their care. It is shocking that we expect teachers, and, for that matter, administrators, not to have strong emotions when students are dealing with personal struggles or even academic ones.

When we go into schools, so many times, even when it is brief, it will be a huge emotional release for the whole staff. It is especially ironic when schools have implemented a new "social and emotional learning" curriculum. Often, we haven't had the training, modeling, or opportunities to do our own SEL work, and you're now expected to teach it? Our curriculum goes so much farther, not only when we do it ourselves, but also when students see us using those skills. We will continue to stress and remind you of the importance of adult applications throughout the book.

RJ is this way of being in relationship and feeling confident enough to risk engaging in conflict. What I want participants to feel is: "this relationship is important," "there is an issue that is bothering me," and "I am going to take a risk and address this issue, and I hope it will make us stronger and more successful in our relationship." These are complex feelings. One of the biggest factors in all this work is the *risk*. If you don't value the relationship, it can be easy to address the little things that bother you because you don't really care about the long-term outcome. If you don't think the relationship will last or be strengthened, then what does it matter how we address conflict? We can yell, we can minimize, we can blame—it is our challenge to care enough and to take the risk to strengthen the relationship.

Like in the rest of life, there are no guarantees. If you attempt to use a restorative approach in your conflict, it won't always work out. Sometimes your students won't trust you, sometimes our colleagues won't hear that you are trying to work together for a better department, and sometimes your supervisors won't see the value in taking accountability or being vulnerable. But if you don't attempt to address these issues, you won't develop trust, connection, or community. And your community will miss out on a great deal of growth.

Simultaneously holding two ideas

Traditionally we would focus on "that is against our norms/rules," and our strategies are all about instilling enough fear or pain to discourage that behavior again. Unfortunately, we've never found a connection between pain and learning. What we find is an avoidance of adults or authority figures, a hiding of mistakes, and a pattern of blaming others. In focusing on punishment we create behavior patterns that corrode accountability and relationships. Often when we think about RJ we recognize that we are trying to hold two competing ideas at the same time.

If we want real behavior change we will need to hold two ideas together at the same time, and create systems that support those ideas. The idea is, "You are valued in our community AND that behavior is not welcome." We seek to make space for accountability and build relationships at the same time.

In traditional systems of justice there is no room for anyone but the youth to be at fault. They are the ones we scold, put in time out, tell them they're bad, suspend, or use other coercive force to scare them into stopping.

One of the beliefs that we hold is that only a tiny fraction of behavior is intentionally hurtful; the vast majority of misdeeds by students (and, for that matter, adults) is accidental or done on impulse. The child who shoves their brother and takes their toy isn't intentionally trying to hurt the sibling, but instead trying to get something to play with. The student who is constantly late to class doesn't do that because they are trying to piss you off (I know I was that kid, sorry Mr Mutier). The student who never brings a pencil or paper to class, yes, they are irresponsible, but no, they aren't in some cabal to take all your pencils and paper. We have to uncouple our ideas about behavior and intention. Other people's intentions are not always as they appear, and despite them feeling deeply personal, they are rarely about you.

However, we know that regardless of intention, actions can have a harmful impact on a person, group, or community. Differentiating between intent and impact is extremely important to this work. Making space for understanding someone's intent is valuable, but making clear the harm or impact of an action cannot be overlooked. Whether it is an unintentional micro-aggression about someone's gender identity or race, or a student throwing a ball that accidentally hits someone in the head, what matters most is addressing and repairing the harm that has occurred. Understanding intentions can help to eliminate shame, blame, and hurt feelings as you move forward together.

9

Equity

We love justice

The fight for racial and economic justice, justice for different genders, and justice at every intersection of our society and culture has been raging for generations. At this point in our history there seems to be an insurmountable desire, interest, and appetite for change. You can see this in the widespread protests, national dialogue, progressive and diverse political candidates gaining momentum and voice, and school reform movements including RJ. It is our sincere hope that we are able to create a more just nation and educational system. Justice and equity are inextricably linked; without one you cannot have the other. We can't talk about restorative justice without talking about racial justice. While these are closely linked they are not the same. We have seen strong RJ systems that overlook or minimize race both in theory and practice, hoping that the humanizing principles of RJ will overcome the systemic racism in our communities and systems. We have also seen strong equity programs that don't include RJ. These systems rely on a "fair" administration of punitive discipline and/or downward pressure on out-of-classroom time. Our belief is that a strong restorative system coupled with a strong understanding of racial equity can begin to eliminate the disproportionality we see in school discipline.

Equity is an outcome, not something that we do. We strive to create *the environment* where equity can arise. Creating the conditions for equity is of such importance that we feel it could be considered the sixth pillar of RJ (see Chapter 2). So let's get into equity. We have different backgrounds and perspectives on this important topic, and although neither of us claim to be scholars or authorities on equity, our work has revolved around this principle for years. So we thought it might be fun to pose three important questions and let you hear each of us respond separately.

1. What do we mean when we say equity?

2. What would equity look like in schools?

3. How does restorative justice promote equity?

Nicholas
1. What do we mean when we say equity?
We need to be careful as we discuss these terms of restorative justice, justice, racial justice, educational justice, equity, racial equity, and finally, cultural competency.

We've talked about restorative justice, but let's break down some of these other terms before we dive too deep. There is a great quote by Cornel West on his website that states, "Justice is what love looks like in public."[1] While I often use this as a great starting point and a way to think about justice as a personal experience, we also need to think about a more academic term. Justice is rooted in the word "just," which means "based on or behaving according to what is morally right and fair." Now we get to more murky waters, morally. "Morally" is informed by our cultural values. But for these purposes let's say "morally right and fair" is when people have "equitable access to life, liberty, and the pursuit of happiness."

So educational justice is when people experience equitable access to educational opportunities. And racial justice is when, regardless of race, people experience equitable access to life,

---

[1]   See www.cornelwest.com

liberty, and the pursuit of happiness. While this goes without saying, people don't experience educational or racial justice.

To put a finer point on the intersection of these ideas—we behave in a just way, systems operate in a just way. While equity is often thought of as an outcome, we have equity or racial equity when, regardless of race or other factors, people have access to life, liberty, and happiness. Justice is a way of being while equity is an outcome from that behavior.

2. What would equity look like in schools?

Racial equity is a huge topic. It shows up across the educational space as well as nearly every aspect of our culture. A couple of examples that might be helpful in the educational space to keep in mind are:

- Our under-representation of teachers of color.

- Our low retention rates of teachers of color.

- Our low participation of parents of color in Parent-Teacher Associations (PTA) and other school organizations.

- Our low percentage of students of color in Advanced Placement (AP) and Gifted/Talented programs.

- Our high percentage of students of color who are being excluded from the learning environment (classroom and school).

The first belief that gets in the way of racial justice is that these outcomes are somehow the fault of students and families of color. You'll hear folks rationalize: "Their families don't show up so they must not care." The historic economic disenfranchisement and incarceration of people of color and black folks in particular created a situation where families need to or are forced to prioritize working long hours over participating in school events. You may hear educators or other families comment about parents or teachers of color and their perceived engagement. If folks of color with little social and economic power surround themselves with folks with lots of social and economic power, they rightfully feel like they don't belong.

Belonging... One of the important experiences for anyone is belonging. If folks of color don't feel like they belong, it is our job to foster belonging. To be clear, if you are the person with social or economic power, it is on you to do the work of sharing power.

Sometimes there is a teacher who is suffering from a debilitating disease like cancer or who has lost a spouse or a child. I have seen teachers band together in the most heartwarming ways, to share sick days and personal days, to pool money to support them through a difficult time, even small things like organizing a food delivery schedule. This is what we do for people who belong—we pool together resources, both social and financial. When teachers of color seem to struggle or become disconnected from the school, it is the responsibility of those with the social and financial resources to offer help, to reach out, and to give grace to those struggling.

It seems we're doing a much better job about understanding the impact of trauma and mental health. We are seeking more understanding, being more gracious and compassionate with folks. Sometimes this is because we can see ourselves having those same struggles, whether it is knowing a spouse or a friend with depression. It might be that we lost a parent to suicide. It might be that we suffered our own trauma, either as children or as adults. I offer to you that folks of color are experiencing something similar, often more intense, and at the same time altogether different. Racial justice for teachers of color is just one of many innumerable educational justice challenges.

As you think about creating restorative systems to support students, remember that this is a mindset. It can and should be applied to your educators' community and family communities as well. While we can speak at length about the many issues that present themselves regarding educational justice, I want to focus on how it relates to discipline.

My understanding of RJ informs the above ideas and possible solutions. I hope you're able to use the framework of RJ that we present here to inform the solutions for many racial justice issues and more human challenges.

While we can speak at length about the many issues that present themselves regarding equity, I want to focus on racial justice as it relates to discipline. Equity is a broad term for fairness, but we want to make sure we are thinking about racial justice as well. When implemented well, we can be sure that RJ will help to minimize and eliminate some of the disproportionate outcomes we see in schools. When black and brown youth experience discipline, it is often in the form of exclusion—exclusion from the teacher's positive attention, exclusion from the classroom, exclusion from the school, and finally, exclusion from the community in the form of incarceration.

When schools do this work well, not only do we see a general experience of inclusion in the daily practice of education, but we also see an experience of inclusion during the experience of discipline.

I know sometimes RJ is difficult—sometimes it blows up in your face and sometimes the outcome is barely positive. But sometimes the experiences in a restorative conference can be a profound feeling of both inclusion and repair. That repair, especially for young people, can be for the victim but it can also be an opportunity for serious repair of self. With that risk of difficulty and positivity I want you to know that I choose RJ over exclusionary and isolating discipline every time.

FINAL THOUGHTS ON EQUITY IN SCHOOLS

I know I don't have the right answer, and I often don't know what to do or say regarding issues of equity. This is all very complex, and complexity always loses to simplicity on social media. I don't have the right answer because there are no right answers. I encourage you to think about two ideas that help me navigate this work:

- Be respectfully curious.

- Do your own work.

These are two concepts that we discussed in Chapter 6 on cultural competency. In short, being respectfully curious is about asking questions, but also following the lead of others. It's about being patient, about waiting to have a personal relationship, dare I say a friendship, before asking what it means, for example, to be black, or Muslim, or white in America. It means asking about a person's humanness before asking about their immigration status. And even while there may be common experiences, refrain from pretending to "know" what they mean or can totally understand. Let it sit with you.

Doing your own work means unpacking some of your acculturated ideas. We all grew up with ideas that now inform how we walk through the world. We have to look at our ideas and at where we find "normal and natural," and be really careful with that. I want to look at every idea where I find myself thinking anyone or any group is smarter, more trustworthy, more righteous than another, ideas that reflect a belief that a person or group is more deserving of love, money, leadership, political power, access, or dignity.

3. How can restorative justice support equity in schools?

RJ is certainly not the only way to support equity in schools, but when it comes to discipline, we've not found a better solution. The deepest challenge is how we take action about events that are harmful and counterproductive to our educational goal, and create an experience of inclusion and support in relation to the school.

If every discipline intervention becomes an experience of inclusion and trust and support, you will see a change in school climate.

If every discipline intervention becomes an opportunity to build trust with an adult in the building, you will see a positive change in school culture.

If every discipline experience is one of learning and account-ability, you will see a change in school culture.

These are especially the case if these expectations are held by black and brown youth who haven't experienced educators as caring or trustworthy in the past.

David

I have spent most of my career in the classroom and working directly with students, and I don't claim to be a scholar or an expert on equity as a larger system—not to mention how intimidating it can be to speak on this topic as a man who has benefited from unjust systems because of my culture, gender, and the way I look. But these are unbelievably important questions to ask, and I am more than willing to contribute my thoughts and experiences to the discussion. To ignore them is a mistake that is all too common, especially by school staff who have enjoyed many societal privileges that their students have not. There are plenty of school teachers and administrators, such as myself, who fall under a combination of some or more of these labels— white, male, affluent, able-bodied, highly educated, cisgender, heterosexual—classifications that may have protected us from the need to directly confront inequity and injustices in our own lives or our school. Regardless of background and classification, we must not shy away from engaging in this discussion for the good of our community as a whole.

When we speak of themes such as equity, justice, and equality, it is important to understand that these are constantly evolving systems that face ongoing challenges. They are ideals and goals to be strived for but are rarely ever achieved for any extended period of time. I think of equity in a school as a garden (yes, I love analogies!). With a lot of work and love and knowledge you can have a healthy thriving garden, where all plants are growing and blossoming. But rarely a day would go by where maintenance is not required—checking the soil, dealing with invasive plants or insects. As gardeners we must constantly check in to ensure the healthy garden's survival. You cannot create a thriving garden and simply walk away until the end of the season to harvest the fruits and flowers. So it goes in school equity. We must be gathering data, having open discussions with students and staff and parents, and frequently asking tough questions of ourselves to ensure fairer systems thrive.

We must first define a vision for our equity work, and constantly and bravely reflect on our successes and failures as we go, and as our community faces new challenges.

Equity can be defined as fair and impartial treatment, and is often conflated with equality. And while these are both noble notions, educators and policy-makers should immediately be able to see red flags in these definitions. We would love to see *fair and impartial treatment* of all students, and yet, it is clearly documented[2] that even the best intentions of educators (often of a different racial and socio-economic background than their pupils) carry implicit bias that against our better judgment skews and distorts how we perceive students, causing us to speak, act, grade, and discipline unfairly. We must uncover these biases, confront them, and create policies to eliminate their negative impacts.

Equality is another beautiful word that can have unintended consequences for our diverse student bodies. Treating everyone as if they are equal is often neglecting the vast array of different talents and struggles that we each face. Although, of course, we should be striving for equality in access to opportunities and resources, we are not, in fact, all equal—no two of us are the same. Acting as such can sometimes only exacerbate inequality by creating one-size-fits-all policies that negatively impact certain groups.

Imagine that a school has built a new state-of-the-art computer lab and has determined that they have enough staff and budget to

---

2   At a minimum, black boys are suspended at three times the rate of white boys (see www2.ed.gov/about/offices/list/ocr/docs/school-climate-and-safety. pdf). In "Are we Closing the School Discipline Gap?," a national review of OCR data in 2015, the Center for Civil Rights Remedies shares that black students' risk of suspension is 30 percent while white students' risk is 13.3 percent, both without disabilities (see https://civilrightsproject.ucla.edu/ resources/projects/center-for-civil-rights-remedies/school-to-prison-folder/ federal-reports/are-we-closing-the-school-discipline-gap).

allow each student one hour per week to use the new facility to do homework, print, photocopy, and get help from tutors there. One view of equality would be to ensure that all students have equal access to this hour of time. But consider that some of the student body may be quite affluent, already having access to technology and tutoring at home, whereas a student who does not have such technology and support may not. For the affluent student the hour in the lab might be unnecessary, and for the students most in need, an hour may be far from enough. True equity in this scenario would be that all students at the school have *a sufficient amount of time with the needed resources* to complete their work. This is not to say that all students will spend the same amount of time working, or achieve the same amount of academic success, but just that no student's opportunity to learn and excel is hampered by a lack of resources. A whimsical and popular representation of this is shown in the image below.

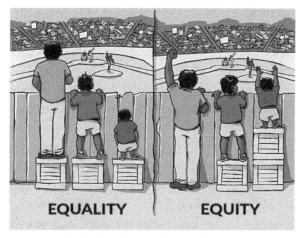

EQUALITY   EQUITY

Source: Interaction Institute for Social Change | Artist: Angus Maguire.

For the purpose of this book we also focus on equity and equality in discipline, something that is severely lacking in schools across the country where students of color, students with a disability, LGBTQ+ students, and other groups are being disciplined dispro-portionately (and unfairly) compared to their peers that do not belong to these and other historically marginalized groups. A more fair, equal, and just way of dealing with conflict is absolutely necessary. And the same work mentioned above would apply— uncovering and addressing bias, examining the racial and cultural identities of staff in comparison to the student population, and creating systems that work to create and maintain the highest level of equity. The same pitfall of "equity" also comes into play. If you have a traditional discipline system based on the equal treatment of all students you might have, for instance, a policy that states three tardies will result in an after-school detention. Sounds fair. But three tardies from a student who is driven to school by an attentive parent may not be the same as three tardies from a student without reliable housing, and having to learn and travel by public transport from each new shelter or foster placement in which they spend time. Learning and considering the context in this example may be more fair than a one-size-fits-all discipline code.

RJ directly addresses these concerns, and we believe it has the power to strive for the most beautiful aspects of equity, justice, and human equality while navigating the pitfalls of these concepts in education.

Can RJ increase equity in schools? We absolutely believe that it can! This can happen in a number of ways, but let's first look at one of the five pillars (or principles) of RJ (see Chapter 2), "Engage all stakeholders." This principle might relate to a restorative circle after a harm has occurred, where not only the author of the act is present, but also community members, allies, invested staff, and family are also present in collaborating a solution and a way to move forward. The key here is about voice—to have equity and justice, all voices must be heard, everyone must share power and have the ability to represent their interests and needs. On a simple discipline level this means that rather than the status quo, which is brown and black students being disciplined disproportionately by overwhelmingly white teachers and staff, RJ circles are held to create spaces of greater accountability, more checks and balances, and a sharing of the process of accountability and healing. Rather than punishments handed down from behind closed doors, this transparency and dialogue to create logical, effective, and collaborative consequences can go a long way to increasing more equitable and fair outcomes in a disciplinary setting.

Of course, this mindset should not just be limited to issues of discipline after a harm has occurred. A truly restorative school will incorporate "Engage all stakeholders" at all levels, valuing family, student, and community input on major policy and curriculum decisions, as well as in disciplinary matters. This is about distributing the authority and placing it in the hands of the student body and community as a whole to prevent bias, structural and institutional racism, and socio-economic factors from disadvantaging certain groups of students while disproportionately benefiting others who are often already at an advantage.

By altering the process of discipline, and even challenging the concept of discipline itself, we can also do a great deal to counteract unjust systems as we work to correct them. While we work to make these needed changes in discipline policy, RJ can immediately work in a positive way by redefining what a discipline referral means. Traditionally it might mean ending up in a principal or dean's office and receiving a lecture or a detention or a suspension from school. If, however, the student ends up speaking with an RJ facilitator or an RJ-minded dean or staff member, rather than a lecture or a mandated punishment they receive a meaningful conversation, a circle of concern and support, a place where they can safely take accountability and learn how to make amends and offer consequential acts of apology, then this referral may become a more positive experience for their support and skill building, an experience where the student encounters adults who truly care and want them in school, and who are willing to listen and help them find a path towards success. In this way, referrals are resulting in extra love, concern, attention, and support. When "discipline" looks like this, you are seeing something far different than the simple statistic of marginalized group X is disproportionately being suspended at school.

RJ is one tool for increasing equity and a move towards increasing the opportunity for academic success for all students regardless of their background, race, and current life circumstances. It is a mindset shift towards relationships, inclusion, and reflection, the conditions you need if equity is to arise and grow.

PART III

CIRCLE UP

10

Circles

Restorative circles are not the only type of restorative practices, and they are not the only way to build relationships or address harm, but they are wonderful tools for accomplishing these goals. In this section we will look intently at best practices for facilitating circles as well as four specific types of circles—relationship-building, accountability, group author, and restorative conferences—and how these can be utilized to build a restorative system that benefits the entire school community.

RJ is a relational approach to conflict. It is not simply a procedure or a buzzword; it is a way of being, a set of values that we walk through the world with, a lens through which we view conflict and, in fact, everything around us. This lens is formed by the five pillars of RJ (see Chapter 2). RJ is not just relationship-building circles or restorative conferences. It is not one thing. These circle practices are simply places where we can practice being human and being in relationships.

It is important to note that not all conflict requires the same level of community response. It would be unsustainable to hold an intensive restorative conference for all of the lowest level conflicts and infractions that occur each day in a school. Therefore we will discuss circles in general, as well as four types of circles that can be employed depending on the severity of the situation and the needs of the community. These four types of circles build on each other and work together to address harm from the lowest level to the most serious across a school community.

Before we jump into these specific types of circles we will zoom out and look at a basic format for facilitating a circle, and cover some general circle philosophy, just to give you an idea of where we are heading. The main sections of a circle format are: Opening; Guidelines, values, expectations; Introduction of talking piece; Check-in; Discussion rounds; Check-out; Closing.

General circle format

1. Opening (ceremony)

As a facilitator you might consider having an opening and/or closing ceremony. This is simply something small that you do or say to officially open and close the circle. It can help set the mood for the circle, mark the transition to and from a circle, and model appropriate and vulnerable sharing. Ideas for an opening ceremony might include: sharing a meaningful and relevant quote, ringing a bell, taking a collective moment of silence for a few deep breaths, or placing a centerpiece.

A centerpiece is simply an item placed inside of the circle, usually on the floor within the circle of chairs. It could be a small plant, a jar of stones, a bowl of glass beads—really anything that gives people something to look at should they need to break eye contact for a moment. Not everyone uses a centerpiece but it can serve several purposes. In a sense it can hold the circle together, as an object on which you can all collectively gaze. It can help demarcate the transition from a class lecture or staff meeting to a circle. In essence the centerpiece says, "This is now something entirely different from what we were doing previously. This is now a special space." It can be an item of significance to the facilitator, and a way to model sharing and vulnerability. It might be an item given to them from a loved one, for instance, and when explained to the group will show that in this new circle space, we can be free to share personal and meaningful stories about ourselves in a way that we might not normally.

2. Guidelines, values, or expectations

These will establish the norms of the circle. You may not need to create these every time you run a circle, but with a new group, this is an especially valuable discussion to have. This can be a quick conversation or a more in-depth one, depending on your needs and the time available.

Expectations for the circle are shared and values agreed. Make sure to have these discussions, and revisit them often, before putting pressure on deep sharing in a circle. And remember that they are expectations of us, not just the kids—we all should be guided by them.

You will hear us (and a lot of folks) talk about "setting expectations." This work might happen when establishing ground rules for mediation, norms for a circle discussion in a classroom, or especially as a set of school-wide values that will shape your entire culture and approach towards mitigating conflict. In any of these cases, it is extremely important that we clarify and provide a restorative framework for how to properly establish these expectations.

In our work with schools, we generally don't spend a lot of time trying to make these expectations "catchy." We don't care if they are inspired by a mascot like "The Flying Eagle's Values" or a slick acronym like GRIT. It's not that we are against these things per se; it's just that is not where the power or effectiveness of expectations comes from. The expectations we operate from at the NC4RJ are: be safe, be respectful, be engaged, be yourself. We find these to be effective at covering what is most important and we offer them as a template to anyone looking for guidance on expectations. But simply having a set of expectations, and plastering them along the hallways, is not nearly enough. So we have created a step-by-step guide for you to think about when implementing school values in your individual circle or your building as a whole.

1. *Develop expectations.* You can use the ones we have just mentioned (be safe, be respectful, be engaged, be yourself), or you can adapt or create your own as a school community or in your circle. There can be a great deal of value in getting input from staff, students, and families (stakeholders) when creating expectations, if your time allows this. But truly, the set of expectations is less important (as they are usually pretty broad and abstract words) than what is contained in the following steps.

2. The key point is "breaking these things down" in your school, creating an opportunity for staff and students to discuss what these things actually *mean to them.* What do they mean in this class, in the hallway, between faculty members, everywhere on campus? For instance, "What does it mean to be *safe* in this physical education class?" "What does it mean to be *safe* in a circle discussion?" Perhaps a counselor discusses what it means to be *safe* in a relationship? Perhaps staff discusses what it means to be *safe* when speaking their opinion at a staff meeting. How do those things show up in our community? Have that dialogue, even if you get statements from folks that contradict each other. Don't shy away from those tough conversations, and keep going until these values are agreed on in meaning and substance.

3. *Make sure not to overlook the discussion about students' expectations of adults.* It is very easy (and common) for adults to lecture students on how they must be respectful in class. They must not swear, they must not wander around the room or put their head down. But respect flows in both directions in a restorative system. Make room for adults to ask their students, "What does it look like when I am respecting you as a student?" You might be surprised and enlightened by some of their answers. If you are at odds with some of their expectations, it is far better to have that discussion explicitly before a conflict occurs. And don't be afraid to model what being authentic looks like. A teacher might explain, "I might not always meet these expectations you have of me. I will try my hardest, but I am only human. If I am not meeting your expectations, I want you to have the confidence and skills to discuss that with me in a restorative way."

    This is really about shifting our expectations to the lens of *us, our, we as a community.* This is *not* simply about an adult's expectations of the student. In a restorative system we are equals as community members, and all deserve the same level of respect and other positive expectations.

4. *Recognizing that these values you are creating do not exist in the abstract,* just to look good on a poster. They serve an actual goal and a mission. Again, we provide our own school mission as an example or template: *Educational excellence for everyone.* We need to keep this mission in mind as we create our expectations, and these expectations need to serve that mission.

5. *Understand that our expectations are often in conflict, and that is okay.* For example, I might carry the expectation of being a great teacher and a great husband and a great father. Being a great teacher may mean staying late one night to help a student in need, but may also result in me not being able to help cook dinner at home. Or we might be asking a

student to *be engaged* and to *be themselves*. But if they are hungry, being themself may mean going to visit a teacher who often gives them a granola bar (and returning late for their class) or may make them disengaged from class as they struggle with obstacles outside of school. We are complex beings with many expectations and needs, which are sometimes at odds. Remember that we can never eliminate human conflict, but we can learn the skills and language to engage in it well, and often emerge from it as stronger community members.

If you have time to create expectations and values together— fantastic. For instance, you might have chart paper or a whiteboard ready to go at the start of the circle, or at any previous time, and say to the group that you "want to come up with values we can all agree on to follow during our circle discussions." Perhaps you start them off with two values that are quite universal: honesty and respect. Explain that it is important to be honest if we are to really connect and to keep the circle safe "we must speak respectfully to one another." Ask if there are other values that people want to make sure are followed during the circle. You can list people's added values along with your own. Some common values that may come up or that you may consider proposing are: privacy ("what is said in the circle stays in the circle") and participation ("you always have the right to pass, but we value everyone's voice being heard"). You can list every suggestion and then go around the circle quickly to see if everyone agrees. It is okay to disagree, and those objections should be resolved before starting the circle.

Expectations need to be established clearly from the start. This is the easiest way to prevent conflict or harmful behavior in a circle. And if unwanted behavior or comments do occur (they will!), you can discuss that in terms of broken expectations, rather than making someone "wrong." This relates to Chapter 4 on non-evaluative language. Rather than saying, "Marcus, stop interrupting!" you can ask, "Marcus, which of our expectations was broken just now?" Do you see the difference there? The second statement is collaborative and more detached, whereas the first is personal and shaming. You can even ask the group the same question in this non-evaluative way: if someone interrupts (or laughs, or rolls their eyes, etc.) during our circle, "Which of these listed values on the board has been broken?"

And always remind the group that *these are truly our expectations*, not the teacher's rules, *because we have created, discussed, and agreed on them as a group.*

3. Introduction of talking pieces

We love talking pieces and could probably write a whole book just about them! But here are some important things to think about when using them.

What is a talking piece? Although it is simply an object that gets passed around from neighbor to neighbor during a circle, this object can have great impact. It helps people recognize authority and power, in themselves, in the activity, in the person who is sharing at the moment. Participation in circles is voluntary, as is sharing, and participants always have the right to "pass." But we have seen how a talking piece can greatly increase the amount of responses given in a circle. It is a phenomenon. Without a talking piece it is so easy to say "pass." Often the next person says "pass" as well and soon the "pass" vibe has spread around the whole circle. But when you are handed a talking piece, you must take a second to hold it, and you feel empowered as all eyes and ears land on you for a moment. You might look down at it and fidget with it as you think. And it is this moment of pause where you are much more likely to share something than to pass. It provides that quick moment of reflection, and there is some honor and respect felt as someone carefully passes it to you and the next person waits anxiously to receive it from you. For these reasons we highly recommend its use in relationship-building circles and even in other circles as well.

WHAT DOES A TALKING PIECE LOOK LIKE?

There really is no perfect example of a talking piece, although some work better than others.

Many people use a small squishy ball as a talking piece. This works because it is a very safe object, even if it is thrown across the room. However, it is also not a very significant object, and by choosing such a safe object you might be messaging a lack of trust or a lack of seriousness to the activity. A squishy ball is not a bad talking piece at all, and will totally work, but we think you might be able to do even better. Think about these fun ideas!...

The talking piece can be something meaningful to the facilitator—perhaps it is a necklace they received from their grandmother before she passed away. In this case, it gives the facilitator a chance to share something personal (why they loved this person), and demonstrate vulnerability and trust in letting other people hold it. It also adds immediate gravity to the activity and often demands respect from even the silliest student (most people would not throw this necklace on the ground in front of the group after hearing how meaningful it was to the facilitator).

The talking piece could be something that relates directly to the community. It could be a small branch (12 inches long, 1 x 2 inches thick, with no sharp points, would be ideal) from a tree outside of the school. David has used this in new classrooms, introducing the piece by saying something like: "This branch will be today's talking piece, the person holding it will be the only one speaking, everyone else will be listening to that person. I took this branch from in front of the school, from a large and beautiful tree I saw. So it will represent this community, the Bronx, a place where I work, but where I don't currently live. In this way it is an honor to be able to hold a piece of it and share this circle with you, as a guest of your community. Thank you for welcoming me." Sometimes, for effect, he will add, "To respect this talking piece is to respect the Bronx; to disrespect it is to disrespect the Bronx. I think that is a beautiful way to think about it."

Logistically a good talking piece will be something that is

easily handled, is not easily broken, and is relatively not dangerous if thrown (although most objects can be dangerous if thrown). Basic common sense applies here. Children will fidget and apply pressure to the object, so it's important not to use something that you value and do not want to be broken if dropped, if you do not think the group is capable of care.

Of all the infinite possibilities, we really appreciate a talking piece that is created by the group itself. Building a talking piece is a great community-building activity. Here are two examples.

Present the group with a stick, like the one mentioned above, but also a pile of colorful strips of fabric (you can cut up some old t-shirts or buy some yarn to cut into lengths of string, etc.). Everyone in the group is asked to pick a color that represents them in some way. Then the facilitator begins (the facilitator should always go first, to model the activity and the depth of response that they are seeking). Explain your fabric or yarn choice: "I chose a blue fabric because I love water, I love to surf and to go out sailing." Then tie the strip onto the wood in a simple knot. The group goes around doing the same. At the end, you all learn about each other's interests outside of school, and you have a very cool and colorful talking piece at the end! You can explain that the piece now has "a piece of all of us," and if someone joins or leaves the group, you can discuss if it is appropriate to adjust or re-do the ceremony of creation.

Another example would be to have everyone take a small piece of paper and write down one strength that they have, something they are good at, or a quality in themselves of which they are proud. Then a container, a plastic jar with a lid, perhaps, is passed around and everyone shares (if they want) out loud their strength and puts it inside. Explain at the end that we all bring different strengths to the group, that we are stronger with everyone, and that the piece of paper represents the best of us.

These are just two examples and it can be fun to ask your group to come up with talking piece ideas themselves!

203

4. Check-in

A check-in is basically just to see how everyone is doing, where their head is at, at the start of the circle, to quickly identify the mood of the group and to catch any issues that may prevent the circle from running smoothly.

This can be a great place to practice SEL. One way is to use "temperature gauge" questions. These are questions that accomplish two things. One, they help the facilitator (often a teacher) get a quick snapshot of how each person is feeling. This can be a great way to avoid conflict or to offer assistance. If someone lets you know that they are having a terrible day or are feeling very angry, this is hugely valuable information if you can then help or accommodate them in some way to avoid conflict in the circle and in the rest of their day. Two, and even more importantly, this helps young people identify their current feelings and express them, a skill that you should never assume that young people possess. It takes time to understand and notice when you are angry or sad or hopeful or nervous. With younger students we have seen success with color charts. Placed up on the board students can see a color next to a word: red next to anger, for instance. Or for the youngest, a color next to a face with an expression such as red next to an angry face. Sometimes teachers will laminate colored cards and leave them in the center for students to take. This is a great small step for students who are not yet comfortable with sharing emotions. Students can say they feel "red" or even just hold up their color card when it is their turn in the check-in round.

For older students or staff, rather than just asking, "How are you feeling today?" you can ask fun questions like, "If your mood was the weather, what type of weather would it be?" You will get obvious answers like, "I feel sunny" when someone is happy, but sometimes unique responses like, "I feel like a tornado of barking dogs." Depending on how the facilitator models the response you can ask for just the weather or a small explanation to go along with it.

Another silly one is, "Describe how you are feeling as a type of ice cream." You will get a lot of folks saying "rocky road" if they are having a tough day, or "vanilla" if it is a boring day, but also unique responses sometimes, like "rainbow with gold sprinkles" or "chocolate chip but the chocolate chips are razor blades."

As always, the facilitator should be the first to share in every round, to model the depth and length of responses that the group should make. For instance, if the facilitator shares "vanilla," most folks will stick to simple answers too (which might be good if you are short on time), but a more complicated response from the facilitator (like "butterscotch caramel fireworks") will encourage the group to get more silly and creative.

5. Discussion rounds

Now that the values and format of the circle have been set and practiced in the check-in round, you are ready to have your discussion rounds, which are usually one to three questions posed by the facilitator, who will answer first and then pass the talking piece around the circle, as everyone else shares and listens. These might be fun "get to know you questions" to build community, or specific questions to address an issue that the group is dealing with, or even questions in response to a recent traumatic event, to provide a space of healing and support.

6. Check-out

This is similar to the check-in round, only now it is to gauge the mood of the group *after* the circle discussion. This might be especially important if you are discussing an emotional topic, or things were said that might have affected the group.

A great question to ask, especially with groups that are new to the circle process, is, "How did it feel to sit in today's circle?" It seems so simple, but we often make a lot of assumptions. You might hear responses that surprise you. And it is a great way to allow people to voice their experience and to demonstrate listening. Remember that this is not about responding to those comments.

It is not about trying to then convince those who did not enjoy the circle why circles are important, and it is not about sharing your excitement with people who did enjoy the circle. It is about just listening and then collecting the talking piece at the end and thanking everyone for their responses.

7. Closing (ceremony)

This is, of course, quite similar to the opening ceremony. A quote, some breaths, a minute of silence—these are all appropriate. It may be removing the centerpiece and putting chairs back into rows. It may be placing, or asking a student to place, with pride, the talking piece back to the special place where it is kept.

Some thoughts on circles, any type of circle, you can consider as a facilitator
Setting the circle

We form the circle by sitting or standing in a circle with nothing between participants as much as the space or requirements will allow. This means that we would usually have only chairs, and there are no desks or large tables between us. This is uncomfortable for many—it can make you feel vulnerable—but it is part of building up our tolerance for vulnerability. We should sit in close proximity; we must encourage folks to get close. As challenging as this can be, building intimacy in the space will go a long way to facilitating authentic sharing.

Adults absolutely need to participate equally in these circles, not as figures of authority, but as equal members of the group. This is what we mentioned about building in equity, even if it means a teacher of 2nd graders sitting in a tiny chair. Very young children are able to answer the question: "Why do you think I am sitting in this student chair with you instead of my big comfy teacher's chair?" "Because you want to be like us," "Because you want to be treated the same" are the type of answers you will often get, and it's wonderful for them to see us in this light, making this type of humble effort to connect. It models the effort we all need to make to get closer to one another in a school setting. With older or more experienced groups, the adult does not need to be the facilitator; this role can easily be performed by a student, and often this will bring great results. We have seen many times that students will pay more attention and respond more authentically to a circle run by their peers.

Circles can also be open to outside participants as guests. An administrator, school aid, or maintenance person or parent can attend, or teachers and students from other classes. This is a great way to make sure that relationships are being formed across a large swath of the community, not just in isolated classroom pods.

Other thoughts

- A restorative circle is not a Socratic discussion, a debate activity, or a place to cover curriculum or content for your class. In fact, this is not a discussion at all; instead you will be *listening* to each other without directly responding. *All circles are listening circles.* This is hugely challenging for some groups and they may need some pre-work to build this skill. Teachers especially struggle with this, as we are used to dominating the airtime in the classroom, and are most comfortable when we feel in control of the group. Letting go of our control (not jumping in to say something) as we relinquish the talking piece to our neighbor can be challenging.

- Participation in any restorative circle should be *voluntary*. As facilitators we should try to find any and all ways to encourage resistant students or staff, listening to them explain from where their apprehension arises. Sometimes you can start with a compromise. It might mean allowing a participant to sit in the room in or outside of the circle, as only a listener. Even if they don't share, they are getting a lot from the discussion, and often actually want to jump in and officially join the group, seeing that it is interesting and/or not scary. Don't force it. Relationships are voluntary. Even after a harm is committed, the restorative conference should be voluntary, although the alternative might be a traditional form of discipline. The student will have the choice.

- Make sure you *recognize how hard and scary and vulnerable the questions asked in community-building circles can be.* We have to ensure safety and participation in a respectful and responsible way. This means going slow, starting with easier, less invasive questions, like, "Who is your favorite superhero, favorite movie, happiest memory, favorite food?" before we jump into deeper prompts like, "Who do you trust in the world, when was a time a friend disappointed you or you disappointed a friend?"

- The *ultimate goal in building communities is to move slowly, deliberately*, one to three times a week (ideally) for the long term. This is indeed a rather large investment of time, but it is an investment that will pay dividends well into the future, not just in class, but in the community at large. And not just in behavior, but in personal growth and academic outcomes.

- If we are not careful we will unconsciously build the best relationship with kids that look and sound like us. (Remember implicit bias from Chapter 6?) This is the problem, why many students of color, or disability or low socio-economic classes feel disconnected and unsupported in schools where the staff are overwhelmingly white and middle or upper class. We, as educators, are not aware of our biases for the most part, and must create systems that prevent them from surfacing unintentionally. *A well-designed circle prevents one group or person from having any more or less authority and voice over another.*

- *We practice equity in circles.* We sit in a circle, and everyone gets a space, a turn, a voice. Everyone, even the teacher or facilitator, sits in the same chair, not the fancy teacher's chair. It's also why we say to students, "No, I do not want you sitting up on the desks or on the floor. I want you to feel comfortable, but I want the message to be clear that no one is above or below anyone else here. We are equals. Your voice matters and you are a part of the community." When done well, this messaging makes a huge difference, and it is a stark contrast to the mindset of, "I am the teacher and you must respect me because I am an authority over you."

- The circle needs to be a *safe space* where the facilitator and participants are genuinely there to listen and learn about each other. Students are amazingly good at seeing through adults and recognizing their true intentions. If the intention is anything other than relationship building (intentions such as controlling classroom behavior or improving performance on tests) the students will see through it. This is not to say that circles have not been frequently shown to improve these outcomes, but intention does matter to their success as a community-building activity. As hard as it is to take ulterior motives off the table, it will serve you well as a facilitator to come from only a place of genuine interest in listening.

- Remember (and share to the group) that all circles are a *listening* activity, and not a *talking* activity. We all want to look good and avoid looking bad in front of others, but if we spend the whole time when people are going around the circle talking, planning out the *perfect* thing to say, we will miss other people's sharing and the point of the exercise. This is also something that needs to be practiced, especially by adults. You can explicitly ask participants to attempt this, not thinking of an answer until it is their turn, and then sharing how that went, what they experienced or realized. This is a great activity.

Many educators deeply understand the importance of relationships and are already doing wonderful relationship building in their schools and classrooms, but we also want to stress that we are trying to build systems that *institutionalize* equity. Circles can absolutely increase equity, but if we leave it up to a single teacher or principal to institute these circles, we are not institutionalizing it. They might do a great job in their space, and so many educators do, even if they have never heard of RJ, but if it's not institutional, it just won't have the same impact on the community. We are working towards systems that say to all community members, "This is what we do here. This is how we relate to each other, deeply and authentically. This is how we repair harm, collaboratively and inclusively."

Key restorative justice tip: Start small
When working with a group that has trouble following the expectations of the circle (specifically, only the person holding the talking piece speaks), you can start really small and build up. See if you can make it around the circle with everyone counting off "one," "two," "three," etc., one after another, as you go around the circle with or without a talking piece. And if you make it all the way around, everyone can clap. Give lots of positive feedback and maybe ask if anyone found it hard or easy, or what they did to respect the rules of the circle (a check-out question). Counting by number should be pretty easy for most groups. Then you might up the ante a bit. What is their favorite food? Or color? This is where things may immediately break down for groups not accustomed to circles. Immediately someone might take the talking piece and say "sushi" and another student might blurt out, "Ew, gross!" as several students laugh.

Rather than getting mad, see it as a teaching moment. First establish the facts in a non-evaluative way. You can pause the circle, empathize that this type of self-control can be quite challenging, and ask someone to tell us what went wrong in that moment where the activity was stopped, or what value was broken, ideally coaching students to take out unnecessary emotion from their explanation. "Suzie said sushi and then Mark said 'ew gross' and a few people laughed" would be a perfect re-telling. Without calling out the student, by speaking generally, you could ask anyone to share why it might be hard not to blurt something out during the circle. This causes students to think empathetically about what just happened, not to just blame a particular student, but to put themselves in their shoes and to try to understand their motivation for disrupting.

Someone might say, "If you really think something is gross or funny, it's hard to hold that in." "Great, I agree," you might respond. Notice that you are acknowledging the challenge and removing shame from what happened. Then you could ask, "How in the world do we hold something like that in, not blurt it out, when we are trying to follow the expectations of the circle? How do we do that, even though it can be hard?" Someone might share, "I try to bite my lip or put my head down so I don't laugh." "That's a great thing to try," you might respond. If it feels safe, you might then directly ask Mark, in a kind tone, "Mark, what was going through your head when Suzie said 'sushi'?" Maybe Mark says, "I had sushi once with my sister and it was nasty, I just immediately felt gross when she said that." "I can totally understand that," you might say, and share a food you think is gross, like mushrooms or liver, or anything you don't enjoy eating.

If Mark seems game, you might ask if he would like to try again and use one of the recommended techniques to keep from blurting out. This is coaching. Consider how this response may be more effective than yelling, "Mark! One more outburst during our circle and you'll get detention." Instead of threatening one student, you are having a learning moment with the whole group, practicing empathy, agency, and non-evaluative language. Then you can try the circle again—after that very public discussion it is less likely that someone else will blurt out in the same way. Often Mark will not blurt out again and will meet the expectations of the circle. At the end, after giving props to the entire group for making it all around, you might ask Mark, "Mark, I notice that you had no problem waiting your turn this time around. How did you do it? Did you use one of the techniques your classmates recommended?" as you publicly laud his effort and allow him to share something that might help others. This is one way to respectfully and openly address small harms (Suzie may have felt embarrassed by Mark's outburst) as a group in a circle.

Obviously the conversation might look different than the example given, depending on how the student who interrupted responds, but it shows the principles from which you, as a facilitator, may try to work.

Relationship-building circles (aka community-building circles)

Many folks have the wrong idea about RJ. They imagine it as simply a response to a harm that has already occurred. Usually they are imagining a restorative conference where the author of the harm faces their community. And while those conferences are important, and will be discussed below, *relationships are the keys to the kingdom*. It is much harder, if not impossible, to do interventions and conflict work if we don't have strong relationships between the students, staff, and families involved. Relationship building is the first step in a preventative pyramid. If anything, the *bread and butter* of RJ are these relationships or community-building circles. Community is one of the most important drivers of behavior. If young people don't find belonging in school, they will find it someplace else, usually a less positive place.

Ideally, students would have the opportunity to engage in some form of relationship-building circle one to three times a week.

If this isn't happening, planning a systemic response to harm will be incredibly difficult, if not impossible. As we head into a conference or an intervention we need to ask, has this student been exposed to these frequent relationship circles experiences? If not, we really need to address that. After all, RJ is all about *restoring relationships.* If there is no relationship to restore, it just won't work.

Relationship circles are a formalized practice of being in a relationship.

Think about that for a moment. We all grew up with a lot of examples of how to be in relationships, how to be friends, partners, collaborators. In an elementary classroom you can see a lot of student behaviors, both inspiring and troubling, as young people struggle to figure it all out.

RJ pushes us to ask interesting questions of students and ourselves that we have often never been asked, with the purpose of articulating and practicing how to be in healthy relationships. We might ask a student, "What makes a good friend?" Many young people can't answer this question—they have never thought about it, despite surrounding themselves with "friends." When an older student reflected on a friend in one of our conferences, they claimed a person was their friend because they got high together, watched the same television shows, and cut class to go to the park. They slowly realized through restorative questions that this person did not support them in their goals, was not there for them emotionally, etc. But this person had not experienced that type of friendship, and was not aware that it could be an option. We need to give lots of positive examples of healthy ways of being in relationships. Sitting in well-run circles are a great way to accomplish this.

A lot of non-traditional schools that we work with do relationship circles really well, as do many special education programs. Students who attend those spaces have often not had great experiences in schools previously and they crave relationships. In restorative schools they get the messaging that "teachers care here," and that is the true key to their success.

A relationship-building circle would follow the main format listed previously with discussion around questions that create space for people to share about themselves and to connect with others. We have mentioned starting with light questions, and slowly over time moving towards deeper and more revealing questions.

Prevention and low-level conflict

If it is not already clear how relationship-building circles can prevent conflict in your classroom and school, consider the power of truly getting to know each other over time in this type of setting. After sharing about something you enjoy doing after school, students may hear others in the class who have the same interest as them, some that may even surprise them. You can even ask at the end of the circle if anyone heard any connections to others in the group. You may get responses like, "I didn't know so many of us like to play Minecraft" or "Amanda and I both love the rapper Drake." As the questions grow in depth over time you might approach questions like, "What is something difficult that you have had to deal with?" Imagine a student who wears a head covering explaining to the group how hard it was to emigrate from abroad and how she was teased when she first arrived. It is likely that most students will not tease her for this after hearing her story. When we know someone, they are humanized and less "other." This prevents many conflicts that arise from fear or a lack of empathy. To address low-level conflict or harm, you might host a circle where you ask a class that has recently become more rowdy, "How does it feel to walk into the class when it is loud and chaotic?" This may help students to self-reflect on their own actions as well as the impact this issue is having on them.

Key restorative justice tip: Airtime
This is *so hard* for many adult facilitators. The key is that *all* people must follow the rules of the talking piece, even the

teacher. This means not responding to students after they speak, while you are not holding the talking piece. This means no "That's a great point, Ohmar," or even saying "Thank you" or making "mmmhmm" noises. We really have to model silent listening when we do not have the talking piece.

Positive psychology!...

After working with an advisory class of students for four consecutive years, from freshman to graduation, David asked them that out of the many activities they did as a group, which one they got the most out of, which would stick with them after graduation. The most popular answer was the "last 24-hour" activity. This is simply a relationship-building circle question that goes like this:

> Name something positive that has happened to you in the last 24 hours.

Like most questions, it is trickier than it may seem. If you had a great 24 hours since the last circle, it is easy to answer. Students might share that they saw a new superhero movie or got paid at their after-school job. But so many teens have difficult lives, and at first the question really troubles them. On the first day David asked this question, there were responses like, "Nothing good happened, I had a horrible night." Totally understandable for a teen who had fought with their parents or broken up with their partner or had even gone to bed hungry. But David explained that this question is a type of mental training, a small slice of positive psychology that teaches us to look for even tiny positive things all around us. He listed some small things, like, "You had a safe place to sleep last night," or "You ate a good breakfast," or "You heard some new music on Spotify that you liked," or "It's sunny and you like the sunshine." Really it was just a fun exercise to try with the group. Students caught on pretty easy and he asked for other suggestions of small good things that might happen to people, even on their worst days. Students offered ideas like:

"You got to see a friend on the bus," or "You have clean clothes to wear," or "Someone made you laugh," or even "Just the fact that you are alive and breathing is a positive thing." For a few weeks this question would come up almost every day in the morning circle and students were quicker and quicker to give their responses. Hilariously, if someone new joined the group as a guest or visitor and they said, "Nothing good happened, it was a horrible 24 hours" the students practically fell out of their seats to ask, "Did you eat dinner last night? Did you have a good sleep? Aren't you alive and breathing!? That's good!" They really started to get the concept, that this activity is not meant to minimize your daily struggles, which may be extremely important and real; it is just to help train your brain to look for even the smallest comforts when you are having a hard time. For some reason, this activity really resonated with some of the students.

Tough kids: restorative justice's secret sauce

One of our favorite aspects of restorative culture is the ability to value the school's most challenging, rebellious, or problematic students. Or maybe you see them as bold, outspoken, and individualistic. Whatever you want to call them, these are the pupils who end up getting a lot of referrals for negative behavior, removed from class, suspended, etc. Ironically, these students often have great attendance, and are often incredibly smart and innovative. That's why they don't just blindly follow the rules; they want to challenge norms and adult authority. Some of these students have notoriously gone on to do great things in life and society. Typically these students do not feel welcome in classes or in the school for a variety of reasons, and have a lot of negative experiences with adult educators. They are frustrated, their teachers are frustrated, and no one knows how to break that cycle. RJ can help!

First, community-building circles can be a place where these students shine more than in traditional instructional settings. It is difficult to be well behaved during algebra class if you don't understand the work and it feels hopeless, or if it is too easy and you are bored, or you have an attention disorder, or any other issue that makes these children *seem* difficult. But a circle is usually very easy to participate in. You might be sharing your favorite food or the music you like, for starters. Often these more challenging students enjoy talking and sharing and connecting, and the circle can be fun for them, especially when there are no right or wrong answers. They can also be given some responsibility, such as choosing the discussion question or facilitating the circle. Sure, some of these students will also struggle with the expectations of the circle and they can be disruptive there in the same way as in a class lecture, but some of the pressures to act out normally (attention seeking, frustration with lack of understanding content, not feeling valued or heard) have been removed. Proper facilitation and some one-on-one support can really make circles a safe space for these students to really be part of the group and gain confidence and value.

If you are lucky enough to have some sort of an RJ office in your school, this can also be a special space to honor the skills of these students. In our work we see a lot of these students in need of support, showing up in the RJ office for minor and sometimes major behavioral issues. But because RJ is all about building relationships, the staff in the office usually form outstanding relationships over time—sharing food, talking about life and the decisions students are making in class, showing loving support while maintaining firm boundaries. When you work in the RJ office, these "high flyers," those frequently in the office, really do become loved. Usually those staff in the office become privy to their private struggles outside of school that explain a lot of the issues with their behavior in class. Over time, as they age and mature, with RJ's support these students can become a *huge* asset in the school and in circles. Many times we have asked these students to sit in on circles with younger students who have gotten in trouble. It can be hard for a young student to hear from an adult that they should not fight, or to stay away from marijuana, etc., but when an older student is there sharing how these choices negatively impacted their life, someone who comes from the same background or neighborhood or who has gone through similar experiences, well, that can be extremely powerful. These students can do things that we, as adults, simply cannot do. With some support, these students can be guest speakers in younger classes, facilitate circles themselves, and mediate small conflicts. Involving students is always powerful, but these students, who are often well known and influential on campus, can really play a huge role.

We hope you can see the other side of the coin. Yes, your RJ program and your circles can benefit from utilizing the skills of students who themselves struggle with behavior or academic success, but it works even more positively in the other direction. By asking for the help of these students, by recognizing their skillsets, experiences and influence in the school, you are honoring them. You are showing them that they are wanted and valued. This can have immense positive impacts on their life and self-esteem, and often pays huge dividends in their behavior in classes. These may be some of the first positive responses that they have gotten in school in a very long time. At the very least, the strong relationship bonds formed in the RJ office can be utilized when the student needs support, intervention, or someone to talk to *before* they act out. When you work in the field of RJ these students often start out as the most frustrating, and by the end of the school year, become some of your most favorite people (who still drive you crazy most days! :) That's love. That's the power of RJ with our most challenging students. They seem challenging from a lens of compliance, but when viewed as whole individuals with a lot to offer the community, only with some additional needed support, suddenly their value can become apparent to all, and most importantly, to themselves.

Accountability circles

We have placed accountability circles on the next level up the pyramid. We often want students to take accountability for their actions. We also hear that people want to "hold students accountable" for their actions. We have discussed this previously (see Chapter 5), but here are some brief notes on accountability to keep in mind as we explore this type of circle:

- Our society does not often message to young people that they should take accountability; adults model the complete opposite. From non-guilty pleas of people caught red-handed to never admitting fault in a car accident, the messaging is clear, *try to get away with not taking responsibility first.* Understanding that this is the current reality will help us understand why young people are not jumping forward to own their actions.

- Owning your actions in schools often leads to punishments. No one wants to be punished, so students try to avoid responsibility at all costs. This makes sense. If students felt they were receiving something else as a result of owning their actions (such as love and support and a chance to repair the harm they have caused, the RJ approach), they may be more likely to play ball with honest accountability.

- We don't believe that you can ever hold someone else accountable; people can only hold themselves accountable. If you suspend a student who still denies any wrongdoing, have you really achieved accountability?

For all of these reasons, accountability circles can be immensely useful. Accountability takes practice, it takes a feeling of safety, it takes vulnerability. These values are all quite difficult, for young and old alike. There is a language of accountability with which many people are not familiar or comfortable. And so we must teach it and practice.

An accountability circle would look a lot like a relationship-building circle, with well-established values or expectations, chairs in a circle and with little else, and most likely the use of a talking piece, except the goal here is to take the strong relationships you have been building with your community circles, and leverage that trust and community to create a safe space for folks to get comfortable with owning their actions and realizing their impact.

Understanding impact is a big part of this, impact as a positive or negative force.

The basics

To open the circle, share the reason you're asking the group to take accountability. The facilitator explains why there is a need for the accountability circle, and what has happened or continues to be an issue for the community.

"What responsibilities can you take regarding the situation?" The facilitator asks each person to share ways that they can own their actions and ways that they might more positively affect the current issue.

"How does that impact our learning environment?" The facilitator asks circle members to reflect on the impact this issue is having.

"What commitments can you make as we move forward?" Sometimes, where appropriate, the facilitator will ask this question, looking for folks to make specific pledges of action.

Note that if you want to follow the outline listed previously, these questions can be used in the discussion rounds.

The basics of accountability circles are simple. Just like with relationship-building circles, start small. Practice this type of circle with a minor issue, rather than with a more serious concern. If you practice with easier issues first, your group will find it easier to be more vulnerable and accountable when something big needs to be discussed.

Perhaps you might start with something like a messy classroom. Even this can be a huge challenge. The question to the group might be: "The room was left messy yesterday afternoon. What is something that you personally could have done differently to have helped leave it cleaner and organized, like we expect it to be?" What looks like a simple question is already very challenging. Perhaps some of the students might be thinking a variety of things, like, "I left my area nice, I should not be a part of this" or "I was the one who left crayons everywhere but I don't want everyone to know that" or "I only threw one piece of paper, Jimmy threw, like, 20!" or "I was absent yesterday, what am I supposed to say, this isn't my fault?" These are all understandable thoughts at any age, and you can see that none of these students would normally be jumping to take accountability for the classroom mess.

The first step is for the facilitator to model how it is done. Perhaps it is the teacher facilitating, and they might say, "Now that I think about it, the end of the day was a bit rushed, I could have left more time at the end of the lesson to make sure that the room was cleaned" or perhaps, "I've been meaning to get some storage bins for our art supplies, but haven't done it yet. Maybe if we had better organized bins it would help students put away the supplies easier." It really should be something that feels true to the person sharing, whatever that is. Remember and be explicit with students, that this circle is not about finding who is to blame, or even blaming ourselves; it is about realizing that each of us has the power to affect any situation, and we are trying to think of ways that we can each step up to make things better for everyone. Students will see that the teacher is thinking about their own actions and impact and sharing honestly—not blaming themselves, not shaming themselves. They are not saying, "This was my fault, I am a terrible teacher." They are simply thinking about the impact and influence they have and how it could have been used for good. Then, with practice, students will begin to understand the activity and start being able to modify their thinking towards holding themselves accountable to the highest standards.

Let's look at the previous thoughts that might be in students' minds, and how accountability circles may help them grow.

"I left my area nice, I should not be a part of this" might later become a share of, "After I cleaned my area, I could have walked around and helped others clean theirs too."

"I was the one who left crayons everywhere but I don't want everyone to know that." Maybe this student will see *everyone* owning something and feel safer saying, "I know that I should have put away the crayons."

"I only threw one piece of paper, Jimmy threw, like, 20!" might become a share of, "I only threw one piece of paper but even that one added to the mess and I could have put it into the garbage without throwing it."

"I was absent yesterday, what am I supposed to say, this isn't my fault?" What a normal thought! And yet a truly practiced student like this might share, "I was absent yesterday, but maybe if I had been in school I could have helped clean up or told other people not to make a mess. I know when I am absent I can't be here to help."

This is all for students to understand that every one of them impacts the community with their actions (or lack of action) and that they are important and powerful players in every moment of the day. Wow, what a realization!

Here is another example of accountability circles at work, a classic example similar to the story shared in Chapter 7. A teacher is absent and returns to get a saddening note from the substitute that the class had misbehaved. Maybe some specific students are even named as particularly difficult during the day. In a traditional discipline system, the teacher or dean or administrator may seek out these named students and give them a punishment, often without discussion. If only this were effective! But it hardly is, in our experience—those same students will misbehave whenever the teacher is absent, regardless of past punishments. This "recidivism" mirrors the high rates of recidivism in prisons, despite year after year of "get tough on crime" policies. You simply can't punish your way to good behavior, especially without getting to the root cause of that behavior and providing safe spaces to practice accountability.

In a more restorative classroom, the teacher could call an accountability circle over this issue. She may ask, "What could you each have done to help the day with the substitute go more smoothly?" Depending on how much practice they have as a class in circles and in taking accountability, this might be easy or quite difficult. Just like the previous example, a student who was well behaved may think, "I didn't do anything wrong." Another student may think, "I was loud but Wanda was much louder." This is all a classic blame mindset. The teacher can explain instead, "This is a coaching moment and we can work together as a class to grow from this experience." She may start by modeling her answer. "I knew I was going to be absent and I could have spent a lot more time talking with you about my expectations while I am out. I also could have made my lesson plan for the substitute something more fun and easy to follow; perhaps the lesson I left was not a good one while I was away." This may lead others to be vulnerable, admitting to running around or being rude, knowing that they will not be formally punished this time. It may spur even the well-behaved students to think of ways they could have been leaders, offering help to the substitute or encouraging peers to stay on task. Then, crucially, this work cannot stop there. The next time the teacher will be out, she can remind them of their personal power, ask them to all commit (in the circle) to something positive they will do while she is out, and let them know that following her return they will again sit in the circle to honestly discuss how the day went and how each person contributed to the day positively or negatively. This is SEL work—this is clearly messaging that misbehavior is not acceptable, but doing so through support and community rather than threat and punishment. If the day goes better, she can use a circle to help students feel pride and empowerment over their growth. If the day does not go better she can arrange more individual interventions with students who need extra support. This may look like one-on-one meetings, meetings involving parents, restorative conferences, and even the use of more traditional forms of discipline that employ logical consequences, if deemed appropriate.

Flip it positive!

You can hold an accountability circle even after something great has happened. To take our previous example, maybe the teacher returns to get a fantastic and glowing note from the substitute. They could hold this circle where students could own anything positive they did to make the day go so well. This is fun and still helps students gain the vocabulary of impact and get comfortable sitting in a circle, reflecting on their own actions and impact in front of the group.

Adults!

Accountability is not as easy as it looks! When working with a particular school on this topic we will often ask someone to name a problematic issue with which their school is currently struggling. Maybe they say "low test scores," "low attendance," "bullying," or "roughhousing in the hallways." No doubt, many of these staff members have been troubled by this issue, and many have found themselves placing blame where they think it is due (rarely on themselves, of course, which is totally normal and human). This is where staff can also use accountability circles, in PD or meetings.

We will ask the staff to form a circle and practice with us. We will go around the circle asking them to each share something that they (not someone else) could be doing differently to positively impact this issue. Blaming others is disempowering to ourselves; it gives our power away. Taking accountability is empowering; it puts power into our hands. And yet we find adults really struggle with this activity. Adults will have a lot of the same defensive thoughts that students do. "I teach back-to-back sections in the Science wing, I am almost never in the hallways to stop roughhousing!" or "I teach PE, I have nothing to do with the test scores" or "Most of the bullying is happening online, that's usually not even during school hours." These are our knee-jerk reactions when we feel like someone is going to get blamed; no one wants to look bad or get into trouble, and we and the kids share the same fears. They often don't feel safe to share something they see as a failure. Maybe their principal is in the circle—will they get into trouble for something they share? Will they look bad in front of their peers? Will they be judged or deemed unworthy of belonging? These are the same fears that students have when we ask them to take accountability after they have caused harm. It's hard!!! But it is much, much easier when you have built a safe and vulnerable community that has practiced this skill.

Usually, no one will take much of a risk until someone else does first. The best results come when a leader, such as the principal, is brave and vulnerable themselves. If they are brave enough not to blame someone else but model accountability, everyone else will feel safe to follow. Maybe they offer, "I was going to make an attendance committee to address this issue, but then I got caught up with all the recent state tests and honestly, I just never followed through; it's been a bit crazy around here, as you all know. I can pledge to make that committee by the end of the month, and I hope some of you will consider joining the committee." Or maybe, "I've been so busy with the new superintendent regulations that I might not be giving the mentorship to some of the new teachers like they need, which could really help them raise student test scores next semester." This shows others that staff can be honest and that we need to work together. It might embolden teachers to share more honestly as they relax and think, "Okay I see we are *all* getting on board with this, I can do this too." Even with coaching, people still find themselves being defensive or placing blame on others in the circles and need help staying on track. But most groups catch on and rise to the challenge quickly. "I have been meaning to call a few of my parents to discuss their child's attendance but it keeps getting pushed to the bottom of my 'to do' list. I can make those calls this week during my planning time," a teacher may then offer. Or "Yes, I think I'm one of the new teachers that could use some mentorship, I will make sure to send an email about scheduling some time for a support meeting. I always try to do things myself but I'm glad there is support out there to help me boost my effectiveness next semester." Imagine the power of a whole staff coming together to own this issue and tackle it as a team, rather than blaming each other, or parents, or just the children themselves. This is how you find collaborative solutions— moving from individual blame to shared accountability.

Why we do accountability circles, especially with relatively low-level issues, is to build our vocabulary of accountability, and to grow more comfortable with ownership and self-reflection. Therefore, when something more serious occurs—a fight, a theft, vandalism, hate speech—and we hold a circle with the students involved, they will feel safer to take responsibility and own their actions, they will know what that feels like already, and they will know that the community is not looking to shame and punish them, but that there is a path to taking accountability, dealing with consequences, and making amends without the relationships they have being lost.

Remember that accountability circles can be very powerful, but they are only successful when you have strong and trusting relationships built on the lower level of the pyramid.

Group author circles

Another great restorative tool is the group author (or multi-author) circle. You might have several students at any point in time who are having the same issue meeting expectations or finding success in school. It would be too time-consuming to hold individual conferences for these mid-level conflicts or issues, and there can also be a benefit in convening them together for a group circle discussion.

Group author circles can also be used to replace traditional after-school or lunchtime detentions. Appropriate issues for this type of circle can include a small group of students who, for example, have been skipping class, have not been turning in assignments, have been disrespectful in their speech to others, have refused to remove headphones or hand in cell phones.

As in all circles, the multi-author circle would look the same (a circle of similar chairs with nothing in between, a facilitator, a talking piece, and invited community members).

Nicholas will often use a format that looks like this:

Facilitator:

- Asks the group to "please turn off all cell phones" (if they are in possession of cell phones).

- Introduces themself as the facilitator or circle keeper— keeper of the process, monitoring time and facilitating.

- Thanks everyone for being here. ☺

- Establishes the basic rules of the circle:

  - The person holding the talking piece speaks.

  - The talking piece moves through every person in a clockwise direction.

  - Each person speaks their own piece (be honest, be engaged, be respectful, be yourself).

- Explains that the goal of a circle is to help provide a space for accountability and repair relationships. Circle conversations are confidential; names, and events leading to referral to the circle, are also confidential.

- States: "We are gathered together this afternoon in a circle made up of youth who were referred to us, because of personal actions for which they are responsible. We will start our session with a values circle...please introduce yourself and share what is an important expectation that you feel we should include. [You could have a list of common expectations or the official school expectations to help this discussion, things like: respect, engagement, safety, etc.] This list will reflect how we will treat each other in this circle and will be agreed on by consensus."

Ideally, your group author circle would include not just the students who were referred but also family or community members who may have been affected by the actions and/or are invested in the success of a referred student.

When expectations and values have been agreed on, the discussion rounds of the circle may look like:

1. To youth: Please tell us the details of the incident that you were referred to the circle for.

2. To the community: What did you think or feel now that you've heard what has happened?

3. To youth: Who do you think has been affected by your actions?

4. And, how do you think your actions impacted other people, the class, or school?

5. To the community: How do you think those actions have impacted other people, the class, or school?

6. Everyone: Is there anything you would like someone here to know?

7. To youth: How would you like us to see you now?

8. Everyone: Is there anything you would like to add?

The facilitator then says, "Thank you to everyone who has taken the time to join us in this circle; your participation has been very helpful."

Remember that these questions are a template that may need to be adjusted depending on your circle and the needs of the community.

You can see that this circle is about understanding issues, communicating, listening, and providing support for referred students. It is absent of formal punishment or consequences, other than the fact that attending the circle means giving of one's time and may occur outside of school hours.

It could be very difficult to hold this type of circle if your school has not also been running community-building circles and accountability circles regularly. It would be hard to feel safe sharing a mistake that was made if you didn't already have strong and trusting relationships. It would be odd for students to have invited community guests if they had not gotten to know them with community-building circles in the past. It would be hard to articulate impact (as in Question 4) if you were not already comfortable with this language from participating in accountability circles in the past. You can really start to see here how each type of circle builds from the others as you go up the pyramid.

Like any circle, there is a bit of an art form, a craft, that you, as a facilitator, will develop over time. And you will be most successful when you are truly coming from the lens of *relationship*, not simply wanting to get your point across or change a student's behavior. The goal here is to model compassion and inclusion while maintaining expectations of excellence for all.

Let's look at some other example questions that could also help you move your conversations forward in a group author circle. After all, unpacking expectations and trying to understand where the breakdown is occurring is paramount. Let's use the example of two common expectations in schools: respect and engagement. In a conversation about respect it can be helpful to discuss this more deeply with students who appear not to be showing respect to others. Good questions here could be:

Respect:

- Tell us about a time when you felt respected.

- Who is an adult in your life that you respect?

- Who is an adult that you think respects you?

For students who appear to be disengaged, you could ask:

- What is something that you are really interested in or passionate about?

- What things do you like about school?

- What problems do you want to work on when you're older, or now?

We hope you can see how this is helping to illuminate the concept of respect and engagement; the discussion may provide an insight into a student's understanding and interpretation of these words and help to keep those concepts relevant as you discuss the issue the student is having. It is as important to truly listen as it is to speak and express the harm that is occurring. It is not about compromising on school expectations, but rather than removing students (exclusionary discipline) with shame and punishment, it is about standing with the student and offering them support and empathy so that they may begin to self-regulate their behavior and find greater success in school.

Restorative (contract) conferences

These are usually smaller circles that are convened to address and repair a significant harm to the community. They are usually the most time-intensive and often the most intense, and are therefore at the top of the pyramid, and are used least frequently. Restorative conferences involve the author of the harm, sometimes the victim(s), and deeply tied stakeholders who were affected or who have a strong relationship with the author. The work here is to illuminate the full impact of the harm, resolve any issues that may still be lingering or that need clarification, and, most importantly, to discuss ways to repair the harm and make actionable plans to do so. These agreements, often in the form of a restorative contract, are called *acts of apology*.

It is often this type of circle, one where people are convened after a serious incident of harm, that people think of, when they are envisioning RJ. But while these circles are important, they are not all there is to RJ. And as we have mentioned, without the other levels of the pyramid in your school, it is quite hard to have successful and impactful restorative conferences. It is a huge mistake to think you can walk into a non-restorative system and simply "drop" these types of circles from thin air, as a replacement for suspension, and have any realistic success with the students themselves or within the staff and community.

These circles, following the same format as all the others

mentioned, are indeed called to address deep harms, and can result in profound transformations in the author as well as for the victim and the community in their healing. But they work based on well-established relationships, logistical capacity, committed follow-through, and a community-wide familiarity and use of restorative language.

This is where we have seen so many restorative attempts fail; folks attempt to pull off some very tricky and high-level restorative circles without the foundation to do so. Take the language of accountability, for example. Imagine that you are holding a circle to address a major act of vandalism or a serious physical fight. If the student being addressed is not accustomed to taking accountability, it may be quite hard for them to accept responsibility, or make any act of apology. However, if they have spent some months or years participating in accountability circles, practicing taking ownership over smaller things, they will know that they are a valued member of the school and it is safe to own their actions, that the community is there to uphold values but also to give them a chance to try and make things right. If they have participated often in community-building circles they may feel bonded to those in the circle and be motivated to make things right and preserve valued relationships, rather than simply becoming defensive, blaming others, and shutting down entirely.

Usually, significant pre-work needs to be done before facilitating this type of circle. For instance, if two students had been in a physical fight, you would not want to immediately throw them into a restorative conference without pre-conferencing with each person involved individually beforehand. The goal in pre-conferencing is making sure that the facts have been established and agreed on, that relevant parties such as family or guardians and school or district administration have been informed, and a possible restorative conference circle has been discussed and agreed to. You will often be balancing the opposite forces of the community's need for a swift response to the incident with the groundwork needed to ensure a fair, safe, effective, and equitable conference. All of this should not scare you away from this important practice. The restorative conference can be a beautiful and transformative occurrence, especially if the lower rungs of the pyramid have been well established. But this type of conference is not one that should be taken lightly, without strong relationships between those involved, respectful facilitation, constant communication, and diligent follow-through when tracking the contracts created.

Proponents of RJ will tout some of the amazing acts of apology that they have seen repair relationships and deter future harm that can emerge from restorative conferences, steps that students have taken to own their actions and to give back to the community they have harmed. These circles can be intense and often tears are shed, by students, parents or caregivers, mentors, and invited guests. This is the ultimate form of, "We love you, you are wanted here in this school and what you did was unacceptable. We want to help guide you through what needs to be done to make things right."

Critics of RJ, however, have often formed their negative opinions based on these same circles being done poorly. This is totally understandable. The harms that call for a restorative conference are the most intense and serious, usually warranting a suspension or even expulsion in some cases. To replace or reduce those traditional punishments with any alternative needs to be seen by the community as at least equally consequential, effective, and respectful of the safety of the entire community.

One thing that we can *all* agree on, and this is often where we agree with skeptics, in these severe cases of harm is that *a good conversation is not enough.* Let's say a student curses out a teacher in front of the class or shoves a teacher or throws a chair across a classroom. If that student is involved in a restorative conference, even if the teacher is present to express their feelings and the circle is well facilitated, even if the student shows remorse and apologizes sincerely, if that student simply gets to say, "I'm sorry, I promise it won't happen again," it is quite easy to agree that this is simply not enough to address the harm committed. And it is often this fear that "students can do whatever they want, and all they have to do is apologize or maybe write a poem or something, and they get to go right back to class as if nothing happened" that lives in the minds of those skeptical to RJ. To a teacher who feels harmed, or who feels that their class was harmed, an apology is simply not enough. Yes, we can show data that suspensions are ineffective at reducing harm, but we also have to demonstrate that the RJ process is more effective, while still being a consequence of seriousness equal to the harmful act (and at least as impactful as a suspension).

The questions we often use in restorative conferences are listed below. These can, of course, be changed to fit the circumstances. You'll find a variety of questions across the RJ community, but they largely follow a similar outline. Before you start creating or editing these questions, we recommend that you try these for a number of conferences. When you get comfortable with the process you'll find yourself editing these on the fly. They are simple and effective questions to ask the author of a harmful act.

- What happened?

- What was the thinking at the time?

- Who and what has been impacted?

- What do we need to do to move forward?

Here are some things to consider when making sure that your restorative conference is well received by the community as a formal consequence.

Involving all stakeholders

To take the example above, if a teacher has been harmed by a student's actions, someone at the conference may think that the student writing some poetry about the event is a good way for them to make an apology. There are cases where this act of apology is acceptable and effective. We love poetry (David has an MFA in Poetry!), and we recognize that writing poems as an act of apology can be a challenging and vulnerable task of serious impact on some occasions. The same goes for making a piece of art, or singing a song in front of a class, etc. But maybe in this instance the teacher would want more to be done to repair the situation. If the teacher is not present at the circle, for whatever reason, they may not be able to say, "Hey, this is not okay, I am not okay with this as a way to repair this harm." That is why it is very important to have stakeholders at the circle and to have a great deal of trust for the process and facilitation. In those cases where this does not happen, a teacher might simply hear: "Oh, that girl who threw the chair? She didn't get suspended; she agreed to write two poems tonight on violence and she will be back in class tomorrow." If this was how the teacher experienced the RJ process after a chair was thrown in class, you can easily imagine how they could feel quite upset and disappointed or angry with this as a consequence. When you have stakeholders at the circle, no one leaves until everyone is satisfied with the agreed consequences or acts of apology that the student will complete to resolve the incident.

Communicating the acts of apology

Sometimes there are some great acts of apology being done by authors, but if the community does not know about them, there can be a lot of conflict with the process. This is the problem when RJ is being done inside of a "black box." For instance, a student who, in response to their actions, might have mediated with the teacher he harmed, might now be meeting with a counselor twice a week after school to discuss their anger, is volunteering at their local community center, and has agreed to help tutor younger students during lunch. But if the community is not made aware of these actions (in some way that adequately meets the needs of confidentiality) there still might be chatter amongst staff and students like: "You know that student who cursed out Mr K? He wasn't suspended; he did one of those RJ circles, and now he's walking around the halls like nothing happened. That's really not fair. How are we supposed to feel safe when students can get away with murder like that?"

Tracking contracts

Find one or more people whose responsibility it is to ensure that restorative contracts are being completed. It is easy for a student to agree to attend after-school counseling sessions, or volunteer in the cafeteria, or write an essay, but what if they don't actually do those things? Perhaps you have an RJ dean or coordinator or a group of staff that share this responsibility. Whoever is responsible, the follow-through is extremely important. And this is not easy; it takes organization, and time! When David was an RJ dean he streamlined the process as best he could to ensure it was accomplished as easily as possible. The contracts he used were quite simple. At the end of a conference there was a single sheet of paper that had no more than:

I . . . . [Student's name] agree to the following actions to repair the harm to the community:

1. . . . .

2. . . . .

3. . . . .

Final due date: . . . .

Check-in date: . . . .

Signature: . . . .

Immediately, David would enter the two dates (final and check-in) into a calendar—that way, every day he could see when contracts were due, or due for a check-in. Usually he would schedule the check-in date at halfway to the agreed-on due date.

It is important to have a final due date to ensure that there is closure to the event for all involved. If there is an agreement to create a piece of artwork, you don't want the student to keep pushing it off from week to week.

It is important to have a check-in date for several reasons. Young people often have difficulty with executive functioning, planning, etc., and need some coaching and support. Even with students who have all the intention of completing their contracts, some might not do so, simply forgetting that they had an after-school counseling session they had agreed to or that some other commitment is coming due. The check-in ensures that the student knows that their commitment is not forgotten and is taken seriously, and that you are there to support them in accomplishing it, but that you will not let it be forgotten or fall through the cracks. Some folks may be inclined to simply wait until the final due date and "catch" the student for not completing their contract. This really goes against the true principle of RJ. Remember that we are trying to be "coaches and not cops" in these instances, and that we are invested that the healing to the community does, in fact, occur as promised. The check-in is a great way to assist the student before it is too late and the deadline has already passed.

Involving community members, especially those skeptical to the process

It is easy to think that the RJ process is not adequate if you have never actually been part of it. The idea of removing some suspensions as a consequence can be very scary to staff, who rightly want to feel safe and supported in their work. Asking them to join some circles, even when they are not directly involved, will usually leave them more invested and understanding of the work afterwards. They need to feel that their concerns are being heard and respected, and they can also be wonderful additions to a circle, as most educators care deeply about all students at the school, even when they may not be directly related to the incident.

We have mentioned that there is a bit of an art form to a restorative conference, like any circle. And the language and look of the circle is similar to others in the pyramid. The idea is to create a safe space where the author and the victim(s) can be heard, where they can take accountability and can collaboratively decide what needs to happen next to work towards repair. The acts of apology seem tricky at first, but after time you will find how you and others can quite easily discover brilliant and positive actions to help repair relationships after conflict. For instance, if a student makes a huge mess in the art room, it is pretty easy to come up with an act of apology that directly relates. Perhaps the circle agrees that the student could clean up the art room after school on Fridays for a month. That might feel good to everyone. Other harms committed may be less obvious. How to repair after a case of bullying or sexual harassment? What about cheating on an exam? What about a racist joke made by a staff member in the staff lounge? This is where experience, involving stakeholders, and working collaboratively are essential. Also, as mentioned in the following story, "Plexiglass punch," using asset surveys can be crucial in discovering a person's abilities and skills that may be of value to the community as restitution.

As some helpful materials we will now include a general list of possible acts of apology to help you get started; the story, which takes you through one specific restorative conference; and some interesting real-world contract items that David and Nicholas have seen in action.

Possible ways for students to repair harm (acts of apology)
These categories help show the variety of ways that people can make acts of apology. Often, multiple acts are included on the same contract.

1. Community service:

    a. Constructive and educational.

    b. Meets community needs.

    c. Student is involved and engaged.

    d. Student has sense of accomplishment when project is complete.

2. Tutoring/academic support.

3. Counseling.

4. Written/verbal apology:

    a. Take account of what the action was.

    b. How did my actions harm others and myself?

    c. Apology for your impact, explain how you're making things better.

5. Essay or written reflection on harm caused:

    a. What was I hoping for when I caused this harm?

    b. How did my actions harm others and myself?

    c. How can I prevent this harm from happening again?

6. Service that is directly related to harm caused:

    a. Presentation to peers.

    b. Poster or artwork to be displayed.

    c. Assist school staff.

7. Participate in an educational session related to harm caused:

    a. Smaller group session.

    b. Reading/reflection educational session.

    c. Interview/speak with others to learn a different and new perspective.

8. Restitution (working to pay back the victim):

a. Financial.

b. Time.

c. Service.

9. Mentoring.

10. Involvement in community or after-school program:

a. Sports.

b. Music.

c. Drama.

d. Writing.

Deep dive on acts of apology

The best actions of apology are collaborative—they are a blend of what the victim thinks is important and what the author can offer according to their strengths and abilities. To clarify again, when we say "acts of apology" we mean actions that can be taken to help repair harm and re-establish a person's positive standing in a community or with the person or people they have harmed. This might be assisting a teacher after disrupting their classroom, it may be baking cookies for a student they insulted, or attending AA meetings for a student who is seen as harming themselves with alcohol. These are just three of an infinite list of actions that can be taken, acts that go far beyond simply saying, "I'm sorry, it won't happen again," or sitting in detention or at home on suspension. The acts can be as simple or involved as the harm dictates and the community agrees on. After years of doing this work and creating restorative contracts, we never cease to be amazed at the creative ways to repair harm that victims and authors propose and agree to. From a female student cleaning her father's motorcycle (documented with before and after pictures) as an apology for making him drive down to the school and miss work after a fight, to songs written and performed on the topic of violence or drug abuse, to older students volunteering to mentor younger students so that they don't end up making the same mistakes. Rather than removing students from school after a conflict, losing their attendance and potential for that time, these acts recycle positive energy back into the school. Imagine a school with a lot of conflicts, where students are constantly suspended or given isolating detentions. It's just one bad situation after another—a loss of attendance and learning, and a lot of anger and resentment, negative emotions that cause negative acts that cause more negative emotions, a vicious cycle.

Now imagine a school with a robust RJ process and a space for authentic acts of apology. Every time there is a conflict, students are volunteering to clean the cafeteria, or create art for the hallways, or speak to younger students about anger, or perform songs during lunchtime, or any number of other positive impacts that leave them feeling proud, not of the harm they caused, of course, but of the way they took action to make things better afterwards—not being held accountable by the community, but rather the community having a space where they can bravely take accountability for themselves without being pushed away. Rather than simply expending energy punishing, time invested in creating opportunities for growth and healing means that much of that effort will be recycled back into the community by empowered students as positive impact activities throughout the campus.

When it comes to meaningful acts of apology, we need to be careful not just to rely on community service. There are infinite actions that can be consequential and effective—writing, mentoring, learning projects, attending community meetings or substance abuse programs, art projects, public performances, leadership opportunities, etc. It is a mistake to fall into the same few actions when creating restorative contracts that work to address and repair harm. Having a variety of stakeholders at the table will help to illuminate the multitude of possible acts of apology, many of which will surprise even the most experienced facilitator or circle member.

Contract follow-through

We also want to talk about follow-through. It is great to get someone to commit to doing something, but are there systems in place to track and ensure that these things actually happen? This falls into the logistics category that anyone looking to implement RJ in their school must address in their own way. The easiest scenario is when one or more people dedicate much of their time to restorative circles and contracts, and hold the task of following up on them. As an RJ dean, David would, as we outlined earlier, always enter the due date of a contract and a check-in date. He would use the check-in date to help support that the student followed through and to catch any issues that they might be having. Rather than trying to "catch" students at the end of their contracts, he would look to coach them towards completing items along the way. Planning is an executive function that really must be taught to younger students. Asking them where they will write down the contract due date, when they plan to complete the items, and troubleshooting issues along the way models a skillset that many students do not have much chance to practice. The due date is an excellent chance to actually celebrate their completion of an act of apology. Again, this is not to celebrate or reward someone for causing harm or acting out. No, this is only to celebrate the acts of repair they may accomplish after that. You can even create certificates for some students with language like, "John Smith has successfully completed his restorative contract." By celebrating the positive actions taken, rather than simply focusing on the negative ones, we try to encourage agency and a sense of belonging. We are saying to the student, "What you did was wrong, but you are still part of our community, and we appreciate the steps you took to make things right as best as you could."

PLEXIGLASS PUNCH

When I heard the commotion, I grabbed my radio and hurried quickly out of the RJ office just in time to see Javier, a junior student, punch in the plexiglass window on a hallway display case. The principal of our high school was standing nearby and several students and teachers had popped their heads out of various doorways to see what was happening. Other support staff and I quickly walked Javier into our office to cool down and began talking with him and interviewing others to piece together exactly what had happened.

The facts of the incident were pretty straightforward and agreed on by all, including Javier. He had been in the Main office and had just been informed that his schedule needed to be changed, apparently for the second time. The school was recently having to make schedule changes to ensure that everyone's credits were on track for graduation, and these adjustments were causing stress to many students during these first few weeks of school. Javier was frustrated about his new schedule and had stormed out of the office, loudly protesting. The principal was standing near the door at the time and followed him out, trying to explain the necessity of the schedule changes. Javier turned to her and ended his loud rant with something like, "Don't even talk to me, you're a b**ch and I hate this f*****g school!" right before turning to the large hallway display case and punching the plexiglass. We were all grateful that this panel was not real glass and there were no injuries to his hand, but the display was damaged. These were the facts. But once we had Javier calmed down in the RJ office, he began to explain why this had happened and, as in many such cases, there were more layers to the incident than it might first seem on the surface.

I love telling people that I work as a "restorative justice dean," a title that I pretty much made up for myself. My official role is simply dean, a position that most people associate with the handling of student behavioral problems and the handing out of traditional forms of discipline, such as detentions and suspensions. The dean's office is where you would go in most public high schools when you were "in trouble." In contrast, RJ is often associated with attempting to find alternatives to these traditional punishments, by holistically assessing a situation, seeing how the root causes might be alleviated to prevent future problems, creating a space for conversation and accountability, and looking for ways to creatively repair harm to community relationships. So, by combining these two titles into one "RJ dean" role, it often made people stop and think. In a school like ours, with a great deal of conflict, the title also captured the complex needs and desires of the school community for emotional support as well as for order and safety. I was proud to be part of this new effort at the school, and grateful that Javier had the time and space to fully unpack his side of what had just happened.

After talking with Javier, it became clear that this incident was not so much about the schedule change, but that he still held on to a lot of resentment from events of the previous year. Apparently, he had made some bad decisions and was not allowed to go on the end of the year field trip to an amusement park. He was heartbroken by this decision and felt that it was not fair, especially because his trip deposit was not returned. Because it had happened right at the end of the year, and before the school had fully began implementing restorative practices, this disappointment had not been resolved for him. Javier told us, through streaming tears, that he had "done so much for this school," had "decorated almost every school dance," and "could not believe they were treating me this way." He felt betrayed by a school, and a principal, he had once loved. The schedule change was just a catalyst at the beginning of the new year that allowed this eruption of anger and emotion.

On the one hand, Javier had clearly broken two of our school's "core values," respect and safety. But it was also evident that the real root of the issue was that his relationship with the principal and the school had been greatly damaged from the previous year. He could have faced a traditional punishment such as detention or possibly a suspension, but that would have probably done nothing to fix the way he felt towards the school community, and his anger and hurt would keep bubbling over into more incidents. It seemed clear to us that we needed to do a restorative conference, a gathering of the relevant stakeholders in the matter to make sure that all people were heard and we could find ways to repair and move forward for good. Javier listed a few staff members, including the principal, whom he associated with the field trip decision, and a friend he wanted in the circle for emotional support. We also invited a teacher and a school secretary/parent coordinator who knew Javier well. In addition, I was there to facilitate the circle along with the other school dean. We did some pre-conference meetings and eventually gathered these people together for the circle.

All participants were aware of the school trip issue the year prior, and understood that before Javier could take ownership of his actions in the hallway, he needed to be heard about this. And so, in that circle, he was heard. All of the staff members involved (I had not been at the school the previous year) stood by the decision to ban him from the trip, but the principal did express that it had been a very hard decision, and one that needed to be made quite quickly on the day of the trip itself, based on a concern for the safety of another student with whom Javier was having conflict. There was not a real resolution here, but Javier got to say how betrayed he had felt and how much he felt he had given to the school. It opened up a touching moment between Javier and the school secretary, where he said, "I always saw you as kind of a mother to me, and after that I just felt like you turned your back on me" to which the woman responded, "Javier, I still love you. Even though I was not happy with your choices, you are young and I know that you still have a lot of learning to do. If you want to help us decorate the next dance I would love to have you be a part of it." The principal stated that even though she stood by her decision of last year, she agreed that it could have been handled better and explained more clearly to him. She expressed how much she liked Javier and all the talents that she recognized in him. The mood of the circle began to soften and it seemed that he could now begin to own his outburst in the hallway and work to repair relationships with these staff members, relationships that he clearly missed having.

Javier was now apologetic for his outburst in the hallway and was asked to list the people he thought were most affected by it.

He settled on the principal, whom he had insulted, and the other students in the hallway classes, whom he had disturbed and perhaps scared. We then went around the circle stating a few positive qualities we each saw in Javier (and he in himself), to help us find areas of strength that he could draw from to repair the harm. I love this part of the circle, seeing a young person receive so much praise at a time where they are also being held accountable for a poor decision; it serves to separate the harmful choices from the essential good of the person. One skill that kept emerging was Javier's artistic ability. This also related to the schedule issues he was having, as he no longer had an art class this semester. He jumped at the suggestion to use this passion to make things right with the community.

To address the damage to the display case, which was currently empty, Javier agreed to design an artistic display. In this way, he felt he would be adding something that would show respect to the whole school. To repair the relationship with the principal, he offered to draw a portrait of her, while sitting with her and talking. The circle agreed to these proposals, set due dates, and scheduled the days after school that he would stay to work on completing these items. I knew this aspect would please some of the more traditionalists on the staff who were still a bit unsure about the effectiveness of RJ. The fact that the after-school work on these items would look somewhat like after-school detentions would help them to see that he was not "just getting away with cursing out a staff member and breaking a window." It would take time for some to accept that the detentions and suspensions of the past were not very effective, and that this new way of dealing with conflict could go a long way in improving the school culture.

Simply put, the work that Javier did to fulfill his contract absolutely blew me away. For the 3 x 6 foot display case he created a colorful diorama of the Hollywood hills, replacing the HOLLYWOOD sign with letters spelling out our school name instead. Each letter was cut from paper and standing up by toothpicks on a large hill made of carefully crumpled construction paper. It was beautifully done. From the ceiling of the case was a collection of white origami cranes hanging in the air from fishing wire. He spent hours working on this, and it showed!

The portrait of the principal happened in one 45-minute session, where Javier sketched her while they talked and she worked on sending emails at her computer. She was satisfied that it did not take much time away from her many responsibilities, but still allowed her to be a part of the RJ process and to reconnect with Javier. The beautiful portrait now hangs, framed, behind her desk.

Story debrief

Javier's behavior was obviously unacceptable, but he was given the space to explain where his anger had originated and to eventually take accountability for himself, repair relationships that he had grown to value over his years at the school, and make acts of apology that were meaningful and had a positive impact. He finally felt that his voice was heard, and to address how he had felt harmed in the past, a key component for him to acknowledge the harm his current behavior had caused. Rather than a simple detention or suspension, his acts of apology directly benefited those harmed, restored his positive connection to the community, and replaced a lot of his anger and resentment with a feeling of pride and belonging. His consequences were just a few examples of the many amazing and effective acts of apology that we have seen in restorative schools. Here are some others!...

- Two students who had a small fight were both in a restorative circle. It turns out that they used to be friends. One question asked was, "What was it that had you become friends in the past?" They both shared that they thought the other person was funny. So they agreed to spend some lunchtime and after-school working with their advisor to create a funny video together, and to show that video during one of their advisories, to show others that they were over their conflict, and as a way to give back to the class their argument had affected.

- A high school student who was caught with alcohol on a school trip organized by the class council agreed to join the class council to give back her time. The next year she actually became president of the council! In this same instance this student agreed to go and observe one AA meeting, accompanied by her parent, to see the impact that alcohol has on other people's lives.

- An older student who was involved in a fight agreed to go to every freshman advisory and host a real-talk discussion on anger and fighting, to discuss his choices and how it had affected him. The student loved the role of mentoring younger students; those students, even the toughest, immediately listened and respected him, and shared their thoughts and questions frankly. It was not always the advice that adults would have shared, things like, "It's just not worth fighting at the school and risking your whole future. If you feel the need to fight someone, do it somewhere else." But the conversation was real and honest, and it definitely made that student feel like his role at the school could be a much more positive one.

- Two groups (cliques) of students that were involved in a fight with each other looked for a common interest during their restorative circle. Many of them liked to rap, but not all of them, so the circle ruled out making music. They discovered that every single one of them liked to play basketball. So they decided the perfect way to show that they were "over their beef" was to play a game of 4-on-4 during the open lunch gym time, in mixed teams, playing alongside one another for a lot of the school to see. This was in addition to several suspensions in this instance, but was still a powerful restorative statement as students who were previously throwing punches were now on the same team, passing each other the ball and giving high fives when points were scored, mixing peacefully for all to see.

- Cheerleaders who were involved in an incident worked to choreograph a routine to address the issue and performed it at lunchtime for their peers to see.

Sometimes the contract item is not directly related. Often during a circle, a teacher will express that even though the incident was not related to their class, the student is currently failing and they are very concerned about their academic success. One contract item therefore can be to attend that teacher's after-school Math/Science/English, etc. tutoring time to complete overdue work or to prepare for a test. This type of item shows that the community cares for the student's success, motivates the student to do something they probably would not have done, and still requires after-school time as in a detention, but with a more direct positive outcome for the student than sitting in a silent detention or study hall. This type of consequence is often agreed on by a circle as a way to restore relationships, but more importantly, to help a student find success in school.

Here is another story that we wanted to include, that utilizes a lot of restorative principles, and that many might find helpful when shifting away from strictly punitive systems of discipline.

THE REVOLUTION THAT RESTORATIVE DETENTION CAN BE

"This doesn't look like any detention I ever seen!" Marcus says about the ring of chairs I've set up for our after-school detention.

I welcome him to the group and ask him to take a seat.

"Welcome," I say to the group, "I am so happy that I get to work with you today. Today we will be discussing some topics, but really it's an opportunity to practice our personal and social skills—skills that help us become successful in life."

As an RJ facilitator at a high school in the Bronx, the staff and I had the opportunity to create an after-school "detention" program that would help reduce the need for out-of-school suspensions and reduce conflict at the school. The goal was to help so-called "at-risk" students identify and explore their intense emotions and often challenging circumstances.

Rather than the traditional style of detention, which seems simply punitive, with students sitting in rows in silence for an hour, I decided to apply my passion for social and emotional learning (SEL)[1] to help reimagine what a constructive or instructive detention might look like.

The approach starts with acknowledging the students as amazing, young works-in-progress, suggesting that they see their mistakes as rich opportunities for introspection and growth, rather than as signs of flawed character. The rapper Tupac Shakur wisely points out that "roses grown in concrete" will undoubtedly bloom with bruised and damaged petals. Rather than focus on student flaws, however, we encourage them to celebrate their tenacity and ability to grow in the harsh conditions that many large cities (and smaller towns across the country) provide.

"Marcus," I ask, "since you are new to the group today, please read the 'Fab 5 of Good Discussions' posted on the wall." Marcus looks at the large colorful poster and reads: "1. Be kind/be respectful. 2. Participate. 3. Ask good questions. 4. One voice at a time. 5. Don't hog the mic."

"Thanks, Marcus, that was well done. These will be the skills that we will practice today. Attempt to use these skills in the classroom, and no doubt you will become more successful in learning and in interacting with your teachers and other students. If you follow these simple rules, you will breeze through any discussion like I know you all can," I say.

Then, "So here's the deal, this is the item we will use as our 'talking piece'—this old wooden spool that I have used for years. This object will help us practice. Anyone may speak when holding this. When you are not holding it, you have to use self-control to

---

1   See https://casel.org/social-and-emotional-learning-and-positive-behavioral-interventions-and-supports

listen and not to interrupt. Why do you think this might this be hard sometimes?"

"Someone could say something mad stupid and you would want to yell at them or hit them," says a student, raising his hand.

"Exactly! Thank you, Brian. It can be hard not to yell out or lash out when someone says something you don't agree with or that makes you angry. So let's give it a try. We are going to start with a simple but proven exercise. I am going to pass this 'talking piece' around, and each person will say only their name, then pass it respectfully to their left." Sometimes this works perfectly, and I ask students to reflect on what went well, what were their observations or thoughts. Many times, the opportunity to show off is too great; someone in the circle will break the protocol. For instance, instead of saying their name, they will make a farting sound just to get a laugh, or they may make a rude comment about a peer's name.

Rather than get upset at this (it's hard sometimes not to!), I smile and try to say something like, "This was a great example of how difficult this activity can be. It can be uncomfortable to sit like this. Some people can handle feeling uncomfortable; other people react to it by making jokes or getting angry. That's why we are here—to support each other, to practice...to grow."

Sometimes a rude comment made can lead to a back-and-forth argument in the group. This is another great learning moment. I may ask, "Can someone tell me what happened after Sarah made that comment to Isiah just now?"

"Isiah got angry and swore at her," commented Brian. "Then she got mad back and they started yelling at each other."

"Exactly! Brian," I say, "that is such a good example of how one comment, made out of turn and in a hurtful way, can cause a whole chain reaction of destructive behavior. We have all seen how simple things like this can escalate into full-blown fights."

This is not a blind assumption. The school population during our 2015–16 school year was approximately 430 students, with more than 300 RJ referrals to the dean's office for behavioral problems. Our school has seen more physical fights than I can count, a fact that dismays me and concerns the administration and the community. We have also dealt with everything from the cutting of classes and long-term absences to drug sales and use, bullying, sexual activity, and weapons use and possession.

The RJ approach means that we try to mediate, hold "fairness councils" (community circles to address harm), and craft creative RJ contracts, including community service projects, connecting families with social services to address the above violations. Unfortunately, we have still had to apply out-of-school suspensions for the most severe violations.

However, I am proud to report that suspensions are usually used as a last resort at our school. I see the RJ after-school detention model as a powerful buffer, working with troubled students and trying to help them develop the personal and social skills they need to remain in school and to deal with life circumstances.

"Okay!" I say. "I've given some of you cards with questions on them.[2] Rather than me asking all the questions, I want to give you a chance to practice number 3 of the 'Fab 5'—asking good questions. Isiah, will you ask your question?"

"All right," Isaiah begins, "it says 'if you were a parent, how would you feel if your child was like you'?"

Several of the students giggle; I remind them to hold their thoughts and comments until they have the talking piece. One girl confesses, "I'd feel mad and disrespected. I'm crazy. I'd wanna beat my ass."

She passed the talking piece and the next girl says, "Yeah, I agree, because I'm not always doing what I should be doing. But I'd also try to be understanding. Like my mom, she doesn't listen, she just straight yells at me; she doesn't, like, ask me how I'm doing or why I did what I did."

The point of the circle is not to give advice. I am there just to listen and ask good questions like everyone else. The productive and fulfilling aspect is that I can "hear" my students thinking out

[2] A lot of people ask me about the discussion cards that I mentioned using. The ones I used were Pocket Ungame® Teens by TaliCor*, but there are many available if you search "Teen discussion cards."

loud about their life and their actions. Usually, I will freestyle the next question based on their responses. In this case I might ask, "Okay, so a lot of you admit that you are often making some bad choices, but that you know your families want good things for you. So, my question is: why is it so hard to do the right things in life?"

Then the talking piece is passed around again. If the topic seems to lose their attention, I'll ask another student to read from their card or to create their own question for the group. I am constantly thanking students for their thoughtful questions and responses, pointing out the courage it takes to share their thoughts and feelings so publicly, and using any outbursts as opportunities for learning.

Naturally, students will often want to discuss how and why they've become part of this unfamiliar after-school detention. If the mood is right, we will pass the talking piece and share what brought us here.

Usually, at least one person in the group will be upset, sometimes justifiably so, and they may share angrily, "I was in class and the teacher told me to stop talking. But I wasn't even talking! So, I cursed him out and walked out of the class. Then he gave me detention! Can you believe that shit. I hate that b**ch!"

It's opportune that I don't need to know whether the teacher was right or wrong about the behavior, because the student's response was absolutely unacceptable. We focus on that. I never argue that a student shouldn't be angry—we all get angry sometimes; it's just how we deal with and express our anger.

First, I'll correct the language that students use as they share in the group. I might say, "Thank you, Simon, I can see how upset this made you, and I appreciate your sharing. Now, before we discuss what happened, let's look back at the 'Fab 5' poster. Number 1 says 'Be kind/be respectful.' Simon was really mad at his teacher today. Instead of calling him a 'b'-word, which is not kind or respectful, how could he have let us know how mad he was without using words that could get him in trouble?" Students are often very helpful in coaching each other; a few hesitant hands go up. "Yes, Sarah, what could Simon have said?"

"He could have just said that it was mad rude the way he came at him for no reason."

"Awesome! I totally agree," I say. "If Simon had just told us that he felt that his teacher was wrong and rude, that would have made his point without breaking any of the rules of the circle and the school. Once you start cursing, most people get angry with you, most people stop listening."

"Now," I say to the group, "Let's analyze and discuss what happened to Simon: the teacher tells him to stop talking; he feels like the teacher is wrong. What might he have done instead of cursing out the teacher in front of the whole class and getting detention?"

I am not explicitly telling him that what he did was "bad"; I am pointing out that there were other options, other actions that would have had different results, results that he may actually have preferred.

A student in the circle offers, "Maybe he could have gone up to the teacher at the end of class and explained that it wasn't him talking, and let him know that he felt disrespected by that?"

"Fantastic! I was thinking the same thing," I say. "I bet the teacher might even have apologized, if he felt he had made the mistake, and he would have respected Simon for approaching him like an adult."

Simon shakes his head. "But that's hard. How am I supposed just to sit there for the whole class after that happened?"

"Simon makes a great point. It would be very uncomfortable for him to sit there, waiting until the end of class to have that talk," I admit. "It would be hard, and it would take a lot of self-control, right? But I bet it's not impossible. I bet if I paid Simon a thousand dollars to sit and wait until the end of class, he could do it," I say with a smile. Simon and the others laugh. They get my point.

"So, that would be hard, sitting in this circle is kind of hard; it's a bit uncomfortable. But sometimes we do hard things in life to get something we want. It might be worth waiting until the end of that class to avoid all that anger and detention."

I continue, "What is another hard or uncomfortable thing you do in life to get something you want? Sometimes when I'm at the gym, I just want to go home and eat cookies instead, but I want to be in great shape, so I keep exercising," I offer. The talking piece is passed around the circle, and students also share things, such as:

I go to basketball practice in the morning, because I want to make it to the NBA.

I babysit my little brother to help out my mom.

Coming to school. I want to graduate, but some days it's hard to get out of bed.

I comment, "Wow, these are really great examples. I think Simon can see how sometimes doing something a bit hard or uncomfortable can actually make his life better. And that's why we are here, to practice that skill. You guys are doing awesome at it. Okay, the hour is almost up. I want to end with shout-outs. Is there anyone who wants to shout out someone in the group that they think did really well at the 'Fab 5' today?"

"I want to shout out Simon," Sarah says. "When I first saw that he was in this group, I thought, no disrespect, 'Oh no, he is going to be crazy and not take it seriously.' But, Simon, you actually did real good and were respectful the whole time."

"Great! Anyone else agree that Simon did well?"

We all put our hands up. Simon smiles a little. I cannot imagine how many times he has been criticized for not doing well in school, and now, in detention of all places, he is being celebrated for doing well. It is unexpected; I hope it will change the way he views himself as a student in our school and as a human being. It may offer him hope that he can grow, can do better, can deal powerfully and constructively with life...even when he gets angry.

I ask all the students in the group to give themselves one point out of five for every skill on the poster that they did well, and to share if they want to how many points they gave themselves. A few students share out to the group why they did or did not give themselves all five points. Together we work towards accurate self-assessment and acknowledge the work that was done.

I've now been an educator for nearly 10 years, and I have a

great deal of respect for the challenges and frustrations of the profession. But educators are sometimes taken aback when I explain that not only did their student participate successfully in an hour-long discussion, but that they were, in fact, a centerpiece—a celebrated success in that discussion!

Simon and many other so-called "at-risk" students have spent too many days, even years, hearing about their "bruised and damaged petals." After dealing with his behavior issues on a daily basis, this teacher may, understandably, have started to lose sight of Simon as an amazing "rose growing from the concrete," to return to Tupac's metaphor.

I am happy that I get to remind fellow teachers, and Simon, that he is exceptional and equipped with all the necessary abilities to become a success in our school and skillful in life outside the school building. It is imperative that we keep working as a community to empower Simon and all students to define and achieve their goals, not simply to comply with the rules for fear of punishment. I am fortunate to work with an incredible group of educators, administrators, and support staff who are deeply engaged in this work of transformation.

Conducting a restorative circle with an ever-changing, multi-grade level group of students who often arrive angry, due to their after-school detention, is not an easy task. But when the dialogue is productive and constructive, and when these kids get to shine at the precise moment that they thought would be nothing but darkness, it is an uplifting and inspirational experience for everyone. This is the revolution that detention can be.

Final Thoughts

Throughout this book, we've been championing restorative justice and practices, which we believe to be an incredibly powerful and transformative tool in building authentic relationships and creating spaces for accountability, particularly after a harm to the (school) community has occurred. In comparison to traditional, punitive punishments, RJ can be far more effective at preventing future acts of harm, increasing equity, and fostering a sense of belonging in young people who all too often simply feel pushed away after conflict has arisen.

Our hope in this book was to impart knowledge from our own classroom experiences, workshops, and trainings, and from the many incredible educators with whom we have worked.

We wanted to share a clear philosophy of RJ, real-world stories of its implementation in schools, and practical tools to help you in your facilitation of positive change in your school culture, beyond simply reforming discipline, and especially for historically marginalized groups. A way to be in relationship with each other honestly, with empathy and a sense of agency, this is the *promise* of RJ. We commend you for undertaking this rewarding but often incredibly challenging and personal work, and we wish you all the best in your journey forward.

Index